To Laila,
Niko + Mo

Be Inspired,

[signature]

A LOUKOUMI MAKE A DIFFERENCE FOUNDATION BOOK

In partnership with the award-winning musical

COME FROM AWAY

INSPIRING STORIES

THAT MAKE A DIFFERENCE

By 75 Kids
Who Changed Their Worlds

HybridGlobal
PUBLISHING

DEDICATION

To our inspiring authors. Thank you for making the world a better place one good deed at a time!

Published by
Hybrid Global Publishing
301 E 57th Street, 4th Fl
New York, NY 10022

Katsoris, Nick
Inspiring Stories That Make a Difference by 75 Kids Who Changed Their Worlds
Hardcover: 978-1-948181-70-9
Softcover: 978-1-948181-71-6
eBook: 978-1-948181-72-3

Cover design: Joe Potter
Copyediting and interior design: Claudia Volkman
Back cover photo: Jillian Nelson

www.loukoumifoundation.org
www.comefromaway.com
Facebook: LOUKOUMI
Twitter: @Loukoumibooks
Instagram: #Loukoumifoundation

All proceeds from this book will benefit the Loukoumi Make A Difference Foundation.

PRAISE FOR LOUKOUMI AND *COME FROM AWAY*

Both Loukoumi *and* Come From Away *inspire us to do good, to be better. Together they can change the world and I am honored to advocate for this wonderful project.*

—*Nia Vardalos*

It was really special to narrate Loukoumi's Good Deeds *on CD not only because of how inspirational it is for kids, but because it was an opportunity to work with my dad. I also loved that it was supporting a personal cause of mine, St. Jude Children's Research Hospital. I am thrilled that the* Loukoumi *books are continuing to make a difference in the lives of children through this wonderful Make A Difference Day program.*

—*Jennifer Aniston*

Loukoumi *the lamb inspires a Good Deeds Movement, encouraging children to make a difference.*

—*Points of Light*

The Loukoumi Foundation and Come From Away's *heartwarming collaboration inspires me to realize our shared mission to change the world, one small act of kindness at a time!*

—*Celebrity Chef Maria Loi*

This story touched the world and celebrates the best that we can all be. It speaks to what people really feel in their hearts. I've seen Come From Away *twice and I'm still very moved by it. We need it especially right now.*

—*Tom Brokaw*

For me the most wonderful thing is to make someone smile and these Inspiring Stories are guaranteed to make children smile all over the world.

—*Gloria Gaynor*

Contents

Chelsea Hynes   *Dashiell Sharpe*

Cooper Jones   *Bennett Knapman*

Liam Vatcher   *Jenna Wright*

Sydney Kellar   *Sarah Pinborn*

Joe Stratton   *Mallory Coish*

Amy Maddigan   *Kaiden Hoffe*

Brady Chaulk-Goodyear   *Kelson Blackmore*

Lily Baker   *Owen Barron*

Ciara Langdon   *Sawyer Ralph*

Ava Clarke   *Ben Barbour*

Sophie Angell   *Graham Pittman*

Foreword

David Hein and Irene Sankoff,
Creators of *Come From Away*

Our musical, *Come From Away*, tells the true story of when thirty-eight planes were diverted to Newfoundland after the US airspace was closed on September 11, 2001. For almost a week, the passengers on those planes were welcomed with open arms. The people of Newfoundland showed them innumerable acts of kindness, and those who were originally strangers were transformed into friends and family.

Since *Come From Away* has opened on Broadway, the show has gone on to play across the United States and Canada, on London's

West End and in Australia. We are so honored to help spread these stories of kindness and generosity around the globe, and we're continually inspired by the new stories we hear along the way. We often reference a line Mr. Rogers' mother shared with him when faced with images of destruction and disaster: "Look for the helpers."

In this collection of stories you'll be inspired by the seventy-five young people who have taken on the responsibility to be "helpers" in ways both big and small. These young leaders teach by example and remind us all that we have the power to better our communities and make a real difference.

It's been a true gift to raise our own daughter alongside the stories of kindness in *Come From Away*—and to read her Nick Katsoris' *Loukoumi* stories, which she's quickly become a huge fan of. And now we can't wait to read this one to her—and to inspire her to try to change the world through acts of kindness.

—David and Irene

Introduction

Nick Katsoris, President
Loukoumi Foundation

When I was a kid, I had a dream. I wanted to be a writer. I will never forget my first-grade essay titled, "Snoopy and the Banana Peel Factory," but even more importantly, I will never forget the encouragement I received from a very special woman. My Aunt Kay was a national Teacher of the Year who inspired thousands of children, including me. She always told me to never give up on my dream and always follow my passion for writing. Although she passed away thirty years ago, she continues to inspire me every day.

All these years later, I never dreamed that my love for writing would take me to this very special place, but that is the beauty of the story—you never know where the road will turn and how your dream will blossom.

I went to law school and clerked for a federal judge after graduation. He was a wonderful man that taught me about how to treat people with kindness. I was inspired to write two legal thrillers based on my experiences, and I thought I was going to be the next John Grisham overnight!

Several years later, I was in the kitchen one night with my wife and I asked her to hand me a box of Loukoumi candy we had been gifted with from Greece. I asked her, "Can you please hand me that box of Loukoumi, Loukoumi?" We looked at each other, and I said, "Wouldn't that make a cute name for a children's book character?"

In 2004, our son was born, and so was Loukoumi. I self-published the first book, simply titled *Loukoumi,* in the now eight-book series about a fluffy little lamb that just wants to make the world a better place. In the spring of 2005, that book about a little lamb, who happens to get lost at the airport while visiting her grandparents in Greece on a summer vacation, was written up in the *New York Times* and hit #4 on the Barnes & Noble children's book bestseller list.

My dream of becoming a writer had come true! I then wrote the second book, *Growing Up with Loukoumi,* which teaches kids the lesson I had learned, that if you work hard and believe in yourself, your dreams can come true. With that book, I started the Loukoumi Dream Day Contest: children submit video entries telling us what they want to be when they grow up, and then we make the winner's dream career day come true.

Our first winner, Sophie, wanted to be a Mars Rover engineer. I didn't even know what that was! I was secretly hoping that she would not win the contest because I had no idea how to make that dream come true. I called NASA blindly and told them about my situation. They immediately responded, loved the idea, and invited Sophie and me to their Jet Propulsion Lab in Pasadena, California, to actually watch the Phoenix spaceship land on the planet Mars.

I couldn't believe what I was hearing. It almost didn't happen because the NASA employee I spoke to originally did not have the authority to offer us this opportunity. But sure enough, that dream day did come true, and when that spaceship landed on the planet Mars, I will never forget the look on Sophie's face.

Since then I have made many dream days come true, and many of the experiences are written about by the kids in this book. Taylor spent the day with Misty Copeland at the American Ballet Theatre; Jordan hung out with Eli Manning and the New York Giants. Lionel played soccer with the New York Red Bulls, Lauren cooked with celebrity chef Maria Loi, and Melina received inspiring words from

Jon Bon Jovi at his JBJ Soul Kitchen. In each dream day, every kid gets that same look that Sophie did with the Mars Landing, that flash of realization that their dream is possible no matter how out-of-the-box it may seem.

During that fateful Mars experience, the Loukoumi road took another serendipitous turn. While I was in California, I had brunch with *Days of Our Lives* actor John Aniston, with whom I had worked on prior charitable projects. John was intrigued by what we were creating and said that he would like to be part of the next book, and without thinking about what I was asking, I said, "How about you and your daughter Jennifer narrating the next *Loukoumi* book on CD?"

Three weeks later, while driving home from work, I received a call from John saying, "Jen will do it!" I almost drove off the road! Later that month, I was back in Los Angeles to record *Loukoumi's Good Deeds* with John and Jennifer Aniston. It is a simple book with a simple lesson that teaches kids to "do something nice for someone today." That line has become Loukoumi's mantra, and the inspiration for the Loukoumi Foundation's "Make A Difference" movement.

Jennifer also introduced me to St. Jude Children's Research Hospital, where we donated the proceeds from that book and several others. This month we are launching the Loukoumi Make A Difference Foundation Treatment Room and Literacy Program at St. Jude, funded by kids' donations.

We released *Loukoumi's Good Deeds* and the companion *Loukoumi's Gift* ten years ago at an event at St. Jude on national Make A Difference Day sponsored by *USA Weekend* magazine. That year we rallied over one thousand children to make a difference with Loukoumi, and today over 100,000 children annually do good deeds.

In 2013 we started our anti-bullying campaign in collaboration with PACER's National Bullying Prevention Center. It started with the book *Loukoumi and the Schoolyard Bully* narrated by Nia Vardalos and featuring the voice of Morgan Freeman as Igor the schoolyard bully. It was also a fortuitous story. I first called Mr. Freeman's office when we were putting together *Loukoumi's*

Celebrity Cookbook featuring favorite childhood recipes from over fifty celebrities. I had a smile on my face for days when Oprah submitted her Corn Fritters recipe, but we had a good laugh when Morgan Freeman submitted a recipe for roast leg of lamb! My dilemma, of course, was how to tell an Oscar winner that you can't publish his leg of lamb recipe in a book about a lamb named Loukoumi? I bit the bullet and called his assistant, and when I told her the reason I was calling, she laughed so hard she almost dropped the phone. That moment created an instant bond, and I felt comfortable enough to reach out to Morgan again. He instantly accepted the role of Igor the schoolyard bully.

Our anti-bullying campaign was a big part of our Make A Difference Day initiative that year, and in early 2014 we received the national Make a Difference Award at a ceremony in Washington, D.C., sponsored by Gannett, *USA Weekend*, Points of Light, and Newman's Own. The award was presented to ten organizations. It was one of the most inspirational days of my life—not only receiving the award from the hosts of the *Today* show, but also learning about and experiencing all the wonderful things done by the other nine award recipients.

That evening, as I took the Amtrak train with my family from D.C. back to New York, I knew that I had to do more. I formed the Loukoumi Make A Difference Foundation, a 501(c)(3) nonprofit that teaches children to make a difference in their lives and the lives of others, and so Loukoumi's path, which was already charitably rooted, took a major turn onto the road of philanthropy.

Since then, we have produced a national television special that aired on Fox stations nationwide, established a good deed curriculum in over three hundred schools, and sponsored the Make A Difference with Loukoumi exhibit at the Westchester Children's Museum. Each June we host the Loukoumi Make a Difference Awards to recognize amazing children and organizations for changing the world.

I have been blessed along this road by many people who have inspired me and believed in what Loukoumi is all about. To the countless celebrities, organizations, supporters, mentors, and my wife, children, and family, I cannot thank you enough. There is no greater gift you can give to someone, especially a child, than to teach them to believe in themselves and inspire them to do good in the world.

I am so honored to partner with *Come From Away* on this incredible book, and I am forever grateful to the creators, producers, and cast for all their support. *Come From Away* epitomizes what kindness is all about and sets the standard for what the world should be like, not just for several days during 9/11 in the town of Gander, but what the world should be like every day.

This book is a dream come true because it unites so many of the incredible kids who are doing just that. They are changing their worlds one good deed at a time through projects that mean something to them and for causes that they believe in. Above all, they are also doing what kids should be doing: having fun in the process. My hope is for these stories to inspire others around the world so the Loukoumi movement can flourish on roads everywhere.

Make A Difference With Loukoumi Day

GOOD DEEDS

"Make someone smile, do a good deed
Lend a hand to a friend in need
Whatever you do, whatever you say
Do something nice for someone today!"

Loukoumi's Good Deeds

NARRATED BY JENNIFER ANISTON

Working to End the Global Water Crisis

Katia Barker

When I was in sixth grade at Sacred Heart Greenwich, the principal of a "sister school" in Africa spoke to my class about the difficulties faced by girls in her country. She explained how significantly different our lives are from theirs. Assigned to a life of domestic chores, many cannot attend school and become trapped in poverty.

Two years later, I was asked to identify a cause I felt passionately about and make a difference by addressing it. Recalling our guest speaker, I chose global access to female education. I discovered that an often-overlooked barrier to female education in developing countries is the global water crisis. With no indoor plumbing, young girls are assigned the task of fetching water for their families, walking an average of 3.75 miles per day to the nearest water source and lugging forty-pound jerry cans home. In addition, many water sources are polluted with parasites and other waterborne illnesses, such as cholera and diarrhea, that kill a child every twenty-one seconds.

I decided to focus on the global water crisis. However, each well costs $12,000, which is a lot of money for anyone to raise, especially a thirteen-year-old with no fundraising experience. During my research I came across a unique organization called Thirst Project, the world's largest youth water organization. In the past decade they have mobilized 2.6 million students to raise over $10 million toward ending the global water crisis.

I signed up with Thirst Project and set a goal of raising $12,000 for one well. I hoped to complete my fundraising by my high school graduation in May 2020. My fundraising activities took many forms, including email campaigns to hosting dances, fundraisers at local restaurants, and selling handmade candles from Swaziland. Thanks to the support of many friends, families, and strangers, I became Thirst Project's largest individual fundraiser, raising my first $12,000 within a year and over $40,000 by July 2019.

In summer 2017 I traveled to Swaziland and saw the effects of my work firsthand. We visited a preschool to celebrate the opening of their new well. The magnitude of their gratitude doubled when we were invited to see their previous water source—a small pond, two to four inches deep, with patches of green and brown water. We watched as a herd of cattle appeared and began to urinate, defecate, and bathe in the water. A teacher explained how the children suffered from worms they had consumed in the water.

My trip to Swaziland was my life's most rewarding experience. Prior to the trip, the global water crisis meant a lot to me, but my knowledge was limited to statistics. Meeting actual people affected by the water crisis and knowing I have helped them is an experience no words could ever describe. I can only hope that I have helped change their lives as much as they have changed mine.

Sharing My Love of Reading

Adelyn Brazil

When my family and I were on vacation in New Orleans when I was seven years old, we walked down a street and saw a beautiful painted book box called a Free Little Library. Since it had books, I loved it from the start! I just knew that I had to find a way to put these book boxes in my hometown of Crown Point, Indiana.

When I got home, I started researching what the costs were to have a Free Little Library. The Free Little Library website gave me tons of information and a way to buy the book stations, but how would I raise the money? Would I ever have enough books? Who should I talk to?

My parents agreed to help me, but they told me I had to do the work!

I put together a business plan and attended the town meeting at City Hall to get my idea of the book stations approved. I was super nervous! I wrote down on paper everything I wanted to say so I wouldn't forget. After all, I was only seven, and being in a room with all those people was pretty scary! When they agreed to my idea, I felt so happy!

I wanted to put the stations in locations where people of all ages could easily get to them, but I also had to think of safe locations. I set up meetings to talk about where the stations could go and let people know I would be taking care of the stations once they were put up. The first station I was allowed to put up was near my elementary school where lots of kids pass by.

Next I needed to find sponsors for my stations who would pay the cost of the station, and they have a plaque on the front with their name. I visited groups like the Lion's Club and the Fraternal Order of Police. I stopped by our local paint store and got a donation of red paint for all my boxes. I also worked with our local printing shop to create a logo I thought fit my book stations: a big bulldog! Our school team is the Bulldogs, and our school colors are red and white. I wanted readers to be able to find my book stations easily.

Once one station was installed, people just loved it. People dropped off more books, families wanted to sponsor stations, and people asked if they could have a book station where they lived!

I created a Facebook page with my mom's help to get more awareness, and soon after I even was featured in an article in the city newspaper! I didn't realize how many donations would come in after that! Because I was just eight, I thought creating a GoFundMe page would be a safe way to accept donations from people I didn't know. It started small, but it got big fast!

In October 2018, I was chosen to be Kid Hero of the month for GoFundMe. A photographer came out to capture pictures of me at work with my book stations. Almost overnight, my goal money amount was surpassed, and there were so many positive messages and donations from people all over the world! I opened a junior investor account at my local bank and continued to work on putting up more book stations.

Right now I have five Bulldog Book Stations in place, and I will soon have seven. I'm also working with others on how to start stations in their towns. I am so thankful for the support of friends, family, and readers from far away! If I never did the Bulldog Book Stations, I would never know how to share my love of books with the world. Making a difference as a kid can be challenging, but I am glad I could find a way to share my love of reading.

"The Smile of a Child"

Michael Colombos

"Come and see our donkey," said the little girl as she took my hand and led me to the backyard. I was happy she was engaging with me and excited that she remembered me from the previous summer. I was at The Smile of the Child in Aegio, a small town west of Athens in Greece. This is a home that fosters forty children who come from abusive homes. The children range in age from newborns to eighteen years old.

My family and I became involved with this charity in the summer of 2017 after we met the man who runs the organization, Mr. Kostas Giannopoulos. He encouraged us to visit and connect with the children in person rather than just raise and send money.

That summer, while vacationing in Nafpaktos, Greece, our family, along with two other families from New York, filled our cars with basic necessities, toiletries, and groceries and delivered them to the home in Aegio. We pulled up to a beautiful, clean home with a nice yard. Lots of little kids ran up to us, all wide eyes and shy smiles. Dora, the woman who runs the house, led us into the main room of the house and the children politely greeted us, brought us a drink, and introduced themselves. They are being brought up with dignity in a house that is, in the truest sense of the word, an actual home for them. There are mother, father, grandmother, grandfather, and sibling figures for all of them. They eat home-cooked, healthy meals, go to after-school activities and get help with their homework. While these children came from difficult, heartbreaking circumstances, this special place was devoted to helping them overcome their situation and helping them thrive.

That fall, we organized a fundraiser in New York at a cycling and yoga studio. We were able to raise enough money to grant these forty children their Christmas wishes for that year, making sure every child got exactly what they wanted! My little sister, Amalia, invited all her friends over and together they made personalized Christmas cards for each child. This has become a yearly tradition.

The following spring I organized a bathing suit drive and sent forty new bathing suits to the kids to use that summer. In the summer of 2018, we visited the home again, and the kids were thrilled to see us. Before we left, we presented the children with new backpacks and school supplies to help make the start of the new school year as great as possible.

A few weeks ago, we sent a box of new shirts and shorts for the children, and this summer we are looking forward to going to visit the children in person again. I have encouraged all my friends and family who go to Greece to make time to visit my friends at this Smile of the Child home or one of their other ten homes throughout Greece.

It is such a rewarding experience to know that I am making a difference in the lives of these children as much as they are making a difference by being a part of mine!

Making a Difference with What You Enjoy

Constantine Katsoris

When talking about how something you have experienced can inspire and motivate you to make a positive difference in the world, there is no better integration than helping others through something you enjoy. Although pursuing good deeds is something people should be attracted to naturally, helping others with something that you are interested in can make charity events and projects much more appealing and successful.

Trying to find something that I could do annually to raise money for needy situations was hard in the beginning. I brainstormed ideas that would make my experience of "doing good" more enjoyable so I could maximize how I affected others positively. Animals and baseball were my biggest forms of entertainment, so I decided to pick projects that would involve one of these two things or benefit them.

When I was eight years old, I decided to raise money for animal shelters by selling bracelets annually on Make A Difference Day. After three years I raised over $1,000 that I donated to the New Rochelle Humane Society. I wanted to help pets in need of supplies and care. I also brought supplies to the Yonkers Animal Shelter and to the animals at the Rye Nature Center, where I am now volunteering.

Baseball is another area of great interest to me, and so in 2016 I organized a baseball equipment drive. We teamed up with the Fordham University baseball team and collected baseball equipment to send to a Jamaican school identified by Ann Torcivia and The Joey Foundation, which Ann formed in memory of her son. He was a wonderful boy who always made others smile, but he passed away at six and a half years old from complications of aplastic anemia.

The Jamaican school had lost its roof in a hurricane, and The Joey Foundation was helping to raise funds for a new roof. I knew it was the perfect fit. We set up a table at a Fordham football game, and with the help of other groups, including Fordham Kiwanis, we collected enough baseball gloves, bats, and helmets for six schools. I then held a fundraiser and purchased sets of bases to go with the equipment.

The school that I donated the equipment to learned how to play the game and created their own "Make A Difference" baseball league.

For the last two years I have continued to make a difference for causes that I love by creating a basketball free-throw carnival-like game in a gym at my local church, Holy Trinity in New Rochelle, New York. I've raised $600 and donated it to various charitable causes.

Through my good deed projects over the last six years, I have learned the importance of combining your charity work with something you love so you can enjoy the experience and maximize the impact it has on others. Doing so has made me enjoy doing good, and I am motivated to continue these projects in the future.

Doing Good Feels Good!

Julia Katsoris

Have you ever experienced the thrill of excitement when you do something good, knowing that it helped someone in need? Doing good can be as little as recycling a piece of trash or donating money to a local charity. Examples of doing good happen every day; you just might not realize it.

On Make A Difference with Loukoumi Day, which occurs on the last Saturday of every October, children around the country are inspired to help others and make a difference. The Loukoumi Foundation holds Good Deed bus tours in cities around the country.

One annual stop is Fordham University. We go to different parts of the school, including the football game, asking people to create a card for a patient and make a donation to St. Jude Children's Research Hospital.

The Loukoumi Foundation is sponsoring a treatment room and literacy program at St. Jude. When children are treated for cancer, they have to be in the hospital for months or even years at a time. They have to miss school, and they fall behind in their schoolwork. The room that the Loukoumi Foundation is funding will help kids to better stay on track with their schoolwork.

Another project is cleaning up the environment. One year we went to Astoria Park and raked the leaves. The leaves we collected were later made into compost and used to beautify the park. When we arrived at the park there were leaves everywhere. Once we were done, the park looked much nicer. When you put your mind to something, you can accomplish anything.

The Loukoumi Bus Tour also went to the Yonkers Animal

Photo Credit: Jillian Nelson

Shelter. We brought food and supplies for the animals, including dog and cat beds, canned food, dog toys, blankets, and more. Giving the animals all of these supplies meant a lot. Everyone tried to make the animals feel loved before they find the perfect home. We didn't just see good being done—we could feel it too.

When you do good, one of your first instincts is to make your idea blossom. One way of doing that is to share your way of looking at things with other people. Once you showcase and display your ideas, it takes what you do to a whole different level. After the bus tour is over, the Loukoumi Foundation holds an event at Holy Trinity Church in New Rochelle where you can showcase your idea so everyone can become a part of your project. Over thirty projects are featured at what we call the Good Deed Celebration.

My friends and I formed a group called the Sweet Treat Girls, and we have raised funds for several charities. People from the other groups support us and we support them, which is what the Loukoumi Foundation is all about. The kindness in that room is contagious, and it makes everyone smile.

Doing good can be a lot of fun, and together we CAN make a difference!

Giving Back

Lionel Li

When I was fifteen years old, I was diagnosed with Non-Hodgkins Burkitt's Lymphoma. I underwent chemotherapy and a transplant (this experience included a relapse). It was one of the longest and most difficult years of my life. I experienced hardships that I wouldn't wish on anybody, but I developed a passion that I wouldn't give up for anything in the world: giving back.

When I was first offered a wish by the Make-A-Wish Foundation before my relapse, I thought it best to treat my family and I to a trip to Disneyland, Paris. However, after my relapse, when I was undergoing the transplant, I had a lot of time to think—about who I was, and who I wanted to be. I was given a chance to reflect on my life at the time and what I truly wanted to do if I survived.

The transplant, while debilitating, gave me perspective, which led me to change my mind. I realized that I shouldn't waste this once-in-a-lifetime opportunity Make-A-Wish was providing—instead I should do something truly spectacular with it. I finally decided to use the wish to benefit a nonprofit organization that had financially assisted my family and I when I was undergoing treatment: Friends of Karen, which provides financial and advocacy support for families with children who are undergoing life-threatening illnesses.

After being declared cancer-free again, I drafted three funding proposals, one for $5,000, another for $7,500, and a last one for $10,000. I sent the proposals to my social workers, and soon was approved for a $10,000 base donation for Friends of Karen's annual walk-a-thon. I knew there was more I could do for the organization

at that point, so I immediately set out to raise additional funds on top of the Make-A-Wish donation. I formed a team, spoke to friends and family for sponsorships and donations, and reached out to my local community in order to raise as much as possible.

This experience was my first exposure to fundraising, and I loved it. I thought about all the children and families the funds would benefit, and I couldn't be more excited to see my hard work pay off. Through this entire experience, I received a wider perspective and developed a much greater appreciation for family, friends, and life in general. I also learned how important it is to make a difference and to help those who need it. There is so much that we can do to help those not only in local communities, but around the world as well. With the proper passion and determination, anyone and everyone can truly make a difference and help create a better world. Loukoumi taught me these things, and my entire experience with Loukoumi has shaped me into who I am today.

The Magic of Goodness

Ava Tsapatsaris

Time is valuable, and when you share your time doing something great, it will definitely be worthwhile! I chose to spend my time doing something that I know will spread the message of kindness and help change the world.

Good deeds and making a difference were embedded into our school curriculum as far back as kindergarten. I clearly remember my teacher reading the book *Loukoumi's Good Deeds*. The kids in class would practice simple good deed gestures, and it quickly became obvious that being kind superseded anything else. Later I became an ambassador for The Loukoumi Foundation. I am also the team captain for Relay for Life, a team with the American Cancer Society.

My Relay for Life project brings communities together to remember loved ones that we have lost to cancer, honor survivors, and raise money to find a cure. In order to support this mission, my team and I took our hobby of making string friendship bracelets and sold them to raise money for the fight against cancer. It was that simple! As an ambassador for the Loukoumi Foundation, I am currently fundraising to build a school room at St. Jude Children's Research Hospital where the patients can learn while they receive treatment.

As you can see, Loukoumi is where it all started for me. It was a book I read as a child, and it inspired me to get out and do good things. I felt the true meaning of what it means to make a difference. I learned quickly that it feels good to do something that helps someone. Many people ask me, "How did you raise money, Ava?" It is easy; I email family and friends, host fundraisers, and sell my friendship bracelets through grassroot events. Honestly, I have fun along the way, meeting new people and spending time with family and friends, all while doing something to make a difference.

Every year we have a successful paint night fundraiser that helps bring our community together to raise money for St. Jude. Being involved with the Loukoumi Foundation has inspired me and others to lead and make a difference. We all are leaders, but we have different ways of showing it. We all have unique ways that we make a difference. Someone can do a good deed by raising money for a charity, while someone else may give a compliment or hold the door open for another person. It's not that hard, and our world needs more of it.

Find what you like to do and create the magic of goodness! A good deed plays a very important part in what makes the world a better place. I always say, "Donating is optional, but finding a cure isn't"—that is my motto. Being part of the Student Council, I was able to incorporate my fundraising ideas at school and encourage others to join me. Every time I fundraise, I get a good feeling; it's like a burst of beaming light, and I know I am making a difference in the world. I encourage everyone to join me in my mission of making the world a better place. After all, what is there left to do?

Photo Credit: Jillian Nelson

Family Fun Packs

Siena Versaci

This year my family and I went to the Broadway show *Come from Away*. We loved it so much, we saw it twice! In the play, the townspeople of Gander, Newfoundland, took in thousands of people who were on planes when 9/11 happened and were stranded at the Gander airport. One of the characters from the play was inspired by the people of Gander and decided to give his employees a day off each year along with one hundred dollars each to do good deeds.

My mom decided to give me, my brother, my dad, and herself one hundred dollars each to do good deeds too. She made us write up proposals for how we would use the money.

I've always felt sorry for homeless people, so I wanted to help them out in some way. I decided that I would most like to help the kids, so we asked the homeless shelter for ideas about what we could do for them.

I came up with the idea of creating Family Fun Packs. A Family Fun Pack is a bin filled with things families can enjoy together—bubbles, cards, water balloons, popcorn, markers, and more. I went with my mom to a store to make the bins. With the hundred dollars, and more money from my mom, I looked for things families would like using together. My mom and I got plastic reusable bins the families could use for other things. I drew a colorful picture to put on each box that said "Family Fun Packs."

My mom and I went to a fundraising party for our local homeless shelter's new children's resource center. We brought the Family Fun Packs with us to give to the families who live at the shelter.

I was kind of scared when I first got there, but soon I saw that everyone was really nice. A lady that worked there showed us around, and it made me see how much people in the community cared. There was a wall decorated by kids all around the shelter. After our tour, I went to the party to see the awards that were being given to the volunteers at the shelter. The people there were all smiling. I had fun hanging out at the children's resource center and seeing what it was like there. After the party, we went back to the shelter, and we took a picture with our Family Fun Packs.

I really had fun and I felt really good about what I did. I want to continue to do more good deeds throughout my life.

The PAWS Project

Molly Wogan

My name is Molly, and I am fourteen years old. I have two rescue dogs named Riley and Gracie. We adopted Riley as a puppy; her pregnant mom had been abandoned at the top of a mountain in Tennessee. Hikers found her and carried her down to have her six puppies, including Riley. We fostered Gracie when she was three years old and soon realized we couldn't live without her. She was abandoned when she was pregnant in Georgia. She ended up in a county shelter after being hit by a car. After having ten babies there, she was about

Photo Credit: GoFundMe

to be put down because she had pneumonia, heartworm, and other illnesses, but luckily she was saved. Once I learned more about what happens to dogs in the South, I wanted to help as a thank you to some of the groups that rescued my own dogs.

When I was twelve, I started a yearlong project that I named the PAWS Project (which stands for Precious Animals, Wonderful Shelters). My goal was to raise $2,500 by hosting tables at events where I would sell my homemade dog toys, treats, and key chains and t-shirts with the logo I created for my project. I also wanted to donate volunteer hours to several shelters. I started Facebook and GoFundMe pages, hoping to show people what happens to dogs in shelters in the South.

Within the first six weeks, I had passed my $2,500 goal, so I changed it to $10,000. I reached that goal in the first six months. By the end of my first year, I had raised $80,000 in funds and collected $40,000 in new donated items from corporations I had written letters to. I spent over four hundred hours raising money and volunteering in shelters in four different states. I even took a trip to Georgia to volunteer for the group that rescued my Gracie. I spent a lot of time visiting local county shelters there and rescuing dogs with the money I had raised. At all of the shelters I visited, the majority of the dogs were being put down. All of these animals were abused, abandoned, and helpless—and all of them deserved a second chance.

I couldn't end the project when the year was up, so instead I made it into a nonprofit that I called PAWS Project Foundation. Since then I have been to Georgia four more times and started focusing on saving more dogs from shelters. We have partners in the South that help us rescue dogs, and we have partners up north to help find these dogs good homes. As of now I have saved over 400 dogs (many of which we have fostered) and raised over $200,000.

With 350,000 dogs entering shelters each year, it will take many people to save their lives. The one thing I've learned is that anyone can help make a difference—especially kids. And even if it doesn't seem like you are doing much, everything adds up and helps makes a difference!

BELIEVE IN YOURSELF AND DREAMS COME TRUE

"Look inside your heart and see,
what it is you want to be.
Doctor, lawyer, movie star,
you an be anything near or far.
Work real hard and don't get blue,
believe in yourself and dreams come true!"

Growing Up with Loukoumi
NARRATED BY GLORIA GAYNOR

An Acquaintance That Will Last a Lifetime

Taylor Beazer

On June 15, 2016, six words rang in my ear all night: "And the winner is . . . Taylor Beazer!" Tears ran down my face. Numbness was all that I could feel, but I wanted to scream on top of the highest mountain. Unbelievably, I was granted the privilege to meet not only my role model, but a legend that will go down in history books as the first African American prima ballerina of the prestigious American Ballet Theatre. This was the day I thought would only be a dream, but thanks to the Loukoumi Foundation, I was able to make this a reality.

The day finally came where I was going to meet the legendary Misty Copeland. On the way there, I began to grow anxious yet excited. *What should I expect? What would I say to her? Would I be able to talk through the tears running down my face?* My mind was racing. As my parents and I waited in the lobby, dancers began to arrive to start their day. I recall thinking about how much talent they each must have to be a part of the American Ballet Theatre and wondering if I would one day also contain such talent.

After waiting for a while, Nicholas Katsoris and his family friend arrived. The artistic director gave us a tour of the facility. We stopped at a classroom, and somehow me and one other person were the only ones in the room with these talented dancers. We sat on a bench watching them warm up, and then reality hit me. I realized that I was in the presence of Misty Copeland, breathing the same air as she was. I had to pinch myself to make sure I wasn't dreaming.

Misty walked over to us and humbly introduced herself, as if I had not spent years learning everything about her. Watching her dance across the floor, I knew why I had been so captivated by her for years. Watching Misty allowed me to fall in love with dance all over again.

The artistic director was kind enough to give us free T-shirts, posters, and a pair of pointe shoes for Misty to sign. Afterward we walked down to the lounge where the dancers usually hang out in between rehearsals. Once again, I saw Misty Copeland. This time I burst into tears and could barely talk. Misty hugged me, took my hands, and said, "It's OK. I love your admiration. It's girls like you that keep me motivated." Never in my wildest dreams did I expect my role model to say that to me. Meeting her made my entire year.

Although that day seemed to pass by quickly, I enjoyed every minute of it. I owe a gracious thank you to The American Ballet Theatre, the Loukoumi Foundation and my parents for allowing me to participate in such a life-changing experience that has inspired me to want to be a role model for others as well. Due to their inspiration, for my seventeenth birthday, I will be going to see Misty Copeland perform at the Segerstrom Center of the Arts in California.

Photo Credit: Jillian Nelson

A Celebrity Chef with a Big Heart

Lauren Berg

Many years ago, I heard about children coming down with cancer, going through chemotherapy, and losing their hair. Upon seeing many pictures of these young children without hair, I decided that I wanted to do something to help these children—something that would make them feel good about themselves.

I went to my temple, Dix Hills Jewish Center, when they were hosting Mitzvah Day. Mitzvah means "good deed" in Hebrew. At this event there were many tables set up for all the children to do various good deeds for others. One of the tables that was set up was from a hair salon. They were measuring eight inches of a person's hair (the minimum length requirement) for them to cut and mail to Pantene to be made into wigs for children.

Since I had long hair, I decided I would have my hair cut so I could donate it to kids who were bald because of chemotherapy. It made me feel extremely good inside because I knew I was doing a wonderful mitzvah. My temple is planning to have "Mitzvah Day" annually, and I am going to donate my hair again. I hope many other kids will continue to do good deeds similar to what I have been doing to make other children smile.

I continued to learn about making a difference through the Loukoumi Foundation. I attended one of their Good Deed events and sold Dove chocolate to help raise money for the Joey Foundation. Soon thereafter I learned about the Loukoumi Dream Day Contest, and I entered by sending in a thirty-second video stating what I wanted to be when I grow up.

When I found out that I won my dream day to cook with Chef Maria Loi at Loi Estiatorio, I was blown away. I have always had a dream of opening my own restaurant and bakery. Winning this contest gave me the opportunity to experience what it would be like to run my own restaurant.

I was very excited to cook with such a famous Greek chef. Chef Maria Loi taught me lots of new cooking techniques. It was a one-of-a-kind experience that allowed me to expand my horizons. She taught me how to be organized in the kitchen and demonstrated skills I was unaware of before. Learning from Chef Maria, I had more fun than I could ever imagine having. My mom was equally impressed. Winning this contest helped me gain more confidence, and I am more comfortable in pursuing my dream.

Winning this contest was not just a dream come true, it was a fantasy come to life. It has also taught me the meaning of making a difference! After becoming part of Loukoumi's charitable Make A Difference organization, I have continued to volunteer with Ann Torcivia of the Joey Foundation and help her sell the chocolates to raise funds for various causes. Together we are making a difference!

Keep Doing Good

Melina Kokkalas

I am the winner of the 2017 Dream Day Contest. At the Loukoumi party, I was sitting at my table when suddenly Mr. Katsoris announced that they would now be viewing some of the Dream Day videos. At that point I got really excited. When my Dream Day video began playing, I saw all my friends looking at me with smiles on their faces. I told myself that it didn't matter if I won—it was following my dream that was important.

The videos kept on playing throughout the party. Then it was finally time to announce the winner, and I held my breath.

"The winner is . . . Melina Kokkalas!" announced Mr. Katsoris.

I started jumping for joy. It was one of the best moments of my life! When he told me what I would do for my Dream Day, I totally freaked out. It completely matched my dream.

My dream is to open up a restaurant and feed people who cannot afford a healthy meal. That is what JBJ's Soul Kitchen does, and that is where I was going. By the way, JBJ stands for JON BON JOVI! They make healthy gourmet food fresh from their gardens and provide meals for people who can afford to pay but also for people who cannot.

As I arrived at the restaurant to live out my Dream Day, I saw a garden in front of the restaurant. It turns out that most of the food they use to cook the meals comes from their own gardens. I harvested crops from the garden and helped serve food to some of the tables.

I loved the idea of this restaurant; I mean, what's better than fresh food from the earth? And then, all of a sudden, a car pulled

into the parking lot and out stepped JON BON JOVI! I gathered the courage to approach him and tell him why I was there. He was very kind and easy to talk to and offered to take a picture with me.

After the picture he told me something I will never forget. He said I should keep doing good and not let anything stop me.

I will always remember his words and this experience, and I hope one day to be on the other end repeating those words to another kid that has dreams of helping feed people who are hungry.

Making the World a Better Place

Grace LaFountain

At a very young age, I learned that I could make a difference in other people's lives. Before that time, I was a typical seven-year-old. I knew that I was a lucky girl, that there were many people around the world that were not as fortunate as I am. I wanted to make the world a better place, but I thought it was impossible for me alone to help people around the globe.

When I was seven, I entered a cooking contest hosted by the Loukoumi Make A Difference Foundation. I submitted a video of myself making my favorite childhood recipe, my Grandmother Hutchins' Famous Fudge. I learned how to create cooking tutorials and posted them on YouTube. I learned all I could about becoming a knowledgeable chef. One night, a month after entering, I received a phone call from Nick Katsoris. I had won! He awarded me with the opportunity to cook with world-famous Food Network Iron Chef, Cat Cora, at her restaurant, Kouzzina, in Disney World. I couldn't wait! It was an amazing opportunity and experience.

When it ended, I used my momentum to help organizations that change the lives of others. I hosted a bake sale, and all the proceeds went to Saint Jude Children's Research Hospital, the Utica Zoo, and Chefs for Humanity, a nonprofit started by Cat Cora. She named me Junior Ambassador, and since then I have been supporting her cause and spreading awareness.

For the last eight years I've had an annual bake sale at the Utica Zoo during their annual Halloween event, the Utica Zoo Spooktacular. I visit all the local bakeries in our area and ask them to donate baked goods for my cause. Several bakeries and supermarkets contribute, and I always have lots of baked goods to sell at the event. To date, I have donated over $5,600 to charity. Over the years, my efforts have educated local leaders about the importance of helping others and its impact on our community. Every year, when going back to the donors, they remember me and before I even say anything, they ask me how much I need from them this year!

I am so grateful that my community is so generous and charitable to my cause. I think I've shown people that it is possible to make a difference in the lives of others, regardless of your age or where you live.

I have learned a lot about the importance of utilizing your abilities to make a difference in other people's lives. Even if it seems impossible to change a worldly problem, you can take the small steps toward making a change. Then, the idea can spread and the support will grow. Several sparks need to be lit in a fire before it can grow larger. It's not about changing the world, but changing each person's world, and making it a little better one step at a time. This is how we, as a society, will improve the world.

Remission Accomplished!

Matteo Lambert

I'm just an ordinary, healthy nine-year-old boy who discovered a love for running after my school's 5K fundraiser last year. A month later I went to a 5K run sponsored by a charity called Hopecam, which is based in Reston, Virginia, near my home. At the race, I met a boy named Fletcher who was the race's honoree. Fletcher had a brain tumor. He was in a wheelchair and had lost a lot of weight. I realized not only how lucky I am to be healthy but also that chronically sick kids can't see their friends. That's where Hopecam helps. It's an organization that

connects kids with cancer to their classmates by using video technology so they can avoid isolation and keep up with their classwork.

In the next few months, my passion for running grew. I ended up running a total of twenty 5K races in 2018. My time went from twenty-six minutes down to a little under twenty-four minutes. Because this is a decent pace for an eight-year-old, I won several awards. After a while, I didn't care about the medals. I wanted to help people through my running. I joined forces with Hopecam founder Len Forkas, who is a world-class endurance athlete. Mr. Forkas started Hopecam about twenty years ago to help his son, Matt, during his battle with cancer. I learned about how he used his strength and stamina in marathons, triathlons, and a bicycle race across America to raise money for Hopecam's support for kids with cancer.

At the beginning of 2019 I started Matteo Runs, a fundraising plan to support Hopecam. Although it has my name, this movement is not about me. I set a goal of running one hundred miles in support of Hopecam's mission to help kids with cancer avoid social isolation. I'm asking for donations while running thirty-two different 5K races in fifteen states. If I can raise $100,000 this year, I can change the lives of over one thousand kids—fifty sick children and their classmates, who also miss their sick friends.

In every race, I borrow the cancer-fighting superpowers of the Hopecam kids. I wear a cape with a picture and the name of a hero with cancer who inspires me. Some people think running one hundred miles is too big of a challenge for a kid my age. Running one 5K race per week is *nothing* compared to what kids with cancer experience. Battling cancer is incredibly difficult as an adult. Can you imagine what it's like as a kindergartner taking medicine meant for people five times your size? It's our duty to make sure these kids don't fight their battles alone. They need to see their friends. Hopecam makes that happen.

Fletcher is now cancer-free, and he joined me at this year's Hopecam 5K. I want all kids with cancer to get better, run races with me, and scream "Remission accomplished" as they jump over the finish line. I am not going to stop running until kids with cancer can be kids!

Dreams Really Do Come True

Sophia Lotto

I want to tell you about a very special dream day that inspired me to help others! On June 23, 2014, I attended a Loukoumi event in New York City. Prior to this I submitted a video talking about what my dream day would be. I wanted to perform on Broadway because Broadway was a passion of mine. I thought there was no way I would win, but then suddenly I saw my video appear on the screen as one of the finalists! I was beyond happy that I would even make it that far! Later in the night they announced the winner of the dream day, and it was me! I was going to be on Broadway!

On September 15th, 2014, my mom, my grandma, and I went to New York City to meet Constantine Maroulis and perform on the stage of *Rock of Ages*! When I first got there, I was so nervous I could barely speak. We met on the steps outside of Times Square. Constantine asked me questions about my love for the theater and why I wanted to be on Broadway when I got older. On the way to the Helen Hayes Theater, we talked some more about what it's like to be on Broadway.

When we got to the theater we went backstage, and he showed me all the costumes and wigs they used during the show. I also got to see some of the actors and actresses that were part of the musical. After this we went on stage and sang "Don't Stop Believin'" by Journey! It felt as though I were actually performing during a real Broadway show! And then Nick Katsoris gave my family and me free tickets to that night's performance of *Rock of Ages*. It was the best night of my life!

Photo Credit: Jillian Nelson

Next I was blessed with the opportunity to be on *Fox 5 News* with Ernie Anastos and talk about my amazing Dream Day experience. On the show we also talked about the Loukoumi Make A Difference Day Special to air the next day. Along with talking about the amazing good deeds many young people had done, the show also highlighted my Dream Day experience.

Being a part of this incredible experience made me want to help my community in more ways. I helped my grandma with a garage sale at her house, and we donated all the proceeds to St. Jude Children's Research Hospital, in addition to funds I raised from a bake sale I organized at school. For the past two years, I have been a team captain for Relay for Life, and my team and I raised $3,000 for the foundation. I've chaired my school's Rock against Cancer event for the past two years. I schedule various musical acts that raise donations from those that come to watch the performances.

Being a part of the Loukoumi Foundation has truly changed not only my life but the lives of countless others! If you believe in yourself, dreams really do come true!

Chasing Tornadoes, Chasing Dreams

Panagioti Pasaportis

Inspiration can come from many things. For me, inspiration came from a fluffy white lamb named Loukoumi and her creator. Loukoumi's creator is probably one of the most inspirational people I have met—and I'm president of my school, so I have met a lot of people! None of them have been as kind as Nick Katsoris. His messages stuck to me like glue! His books spoke of believing in yourself and doing good deeds.

I met Nick Katsoris a few years ago when I entered the Loukoumi Dream Day Contest. The contest offered me the opportunity to experience a day at my dream job. When I grow up I want to be a meteorologist, specifically a storm chaser! I've watched many documentaries on tornadoes, super cells, and hurricanes. Every time there was a bad storm, I would stare out the window and record the lightning and thunder. I'd pretend I was tracking the storm. When I won the contest, I had an amazing opportunity to meet Nick Gregory and Ernie Anastos at the Fox 5 Weather station.

Nick Gregory is a great mentor. He is very kind and patient. I learned about the polar vortex and how to track storms. I got to see several monitors and satellites. I was able to sit backstage and watch a live weather forecast. But most importantly, I was encouraged to believe in myself and chase my dreams (just like chasing a tornado!). I'll never forget that amazing day. It made me feel a need to give back and encourage others. I wanted to inspire others like Nick Katsoris and Nick Gregory inspired me.

I had an idea about how to encourage my classmates to make

a difference. For Halloween I decided to give loom bracelets to my class instead of candy. Not only was I making parents and dentists happy, I was helping a good cause. You see, these were not just any loom bracelets. They were made by Dean, a friend who then sold these bracelets to raise money for the New Rochelle Humane Society. We purchased about thirty bracelets, and my mom and I made special packages for them. I added Loukoumi's message to the package: "Make someone smile, do a good deed, lend a hand to a friend in need. Whatever you do, whatever you say, do something nice for someone today." I spoke to my classmates about kindness and how doing something small can make a big difference.

Kindness is contagious, and if we all do something good, we can make a huge impact.

Photo Credit: Jillian Nelson

Living My Dream (Day)

Jordan Stewart

It was a hot summer day in August of 2015. The sun was beating down my neck and sweat dripped from my chin. I can still hear the whistles blowing through the humid air. I was at football practice. We had just started team scrimmage. Two plays in, the defense got an interception and the offense was coming in. Down . . . Set . . . Hike! The ball came to me and I caught it. As I turned around to run up field, the safety swooped down. *Crack!* I felt numb. I couldn't get up. I wasn't in pain, but I knew something was wrong.

That night, after hours spent in the ER, the doctor told me I had a fractured left tibia and torn meniscus that needed surgery. He also said that I would be out for the rest of the season. I started to cry, thinking, *Why me? Why did this happen?*

Several months prior, I had submitted a video to the Loukoumi Dream Day Contest expressing my dream of becoming a professional football player in the NFL. I didn't think anything of it at the time, but surprisingly I won! For my Dream Day NFL experience, I went to the New York Giants practice facility decked out in my Giants gear, including my favorite Beckham Jr. jersey, and I got to watch the team practice from the VIP section with the players' families! Without realizing it, I happened to be standing next to Odell Beckham Sr., who noticed my jersey as well as my crutches. We chatted about football, and he encouraged me to continue to pursue my dream in spite of my injury. He also brought me over to meet my favorite player, Odell Beckham Jr., at the end of practice!

I also had the honor of meeting and receiving some inspiring words from Giants' quarterback Eli Manning, as well as other players from Big Blue. They took pictures with me and even signed a football I had brought with me! That was a very special day for me. My dream day with the New York Giants encouraged me to pay it forward by giving someone else a chance to live out their dreams in spite of their obstacles.

Since my Loukoumi Dream Day, I have healed well enough to return to playing football throughout high school. I volunteer whenever I can by helping to coach other kids at football camp. I have also participated twice in the Polar Plunge with my teammates to support those with intellectual and/or physical disabilities to train and participate in the Special Olympics. So far I've raised $800 to send two athletes to the Olympics, running into the freezing waters of the Long Island Sound to show my support. It feels really good to help support other promising athletes like myself. It reminds me of how I felt during my Dream Day, and this time, I gave two people a chance to live out their dreams!

Photo Credit: Jillian Nelson

THE PERFECT GIFT

"A gift is a thought your heart creates and need not cost a penny.
A gift can be anything that you wish, made for one or many.
A thoughtful act, a handmade card, a delicious cookie or cake,
the perfect gift is straight from the heart,
whatever it is you make!"

Loukoumi's Gift

NARRATED BY JOHN ANISTON

The Sweet Treat Girls

Julia Katsoris, Melina Kokkalas, Taylor Naclerio,
Madeleine O'Connor, Caitlin Savitt, Lucy Skipper, Siena Versaci

Hi, I'm Caitlin,
I'm Julia,
I'm Lucy,
I'm Madeleine,
I'm Melina,
I'm Siena,
I'm Taylor . . . and we are the Sweet Treat Girls!

"Making a difference" means helping others to make the world a better place. We love to bake, and several years ago on Make A Difference with Loukoumi Day, we decided to hold a bake sale to raise money

for our favorite charities. It was amazing! We baked brownies, muffins, chocolate-covered pretzels, cookies, chocolate-covered strawberries, and together we made almost one hundred cupcakes. We sold our items at the Loukoumi Good Deed Celebration held each year at Holy Trinity Church in New Rochelle. That first year we sold out and raised over $330, which we donated to St. Jude Children's Research Hospital.

The following year we did it again and raised funds for Jon Bon Jovi's JBJ Soul Kitchen, a great organization that helps provide a delicious meal to people who may not necessarily be able to afford going to a restaurant.

We had so much fun that we wanted to do more. Our school, the Anne Hutchinson School, wanted to make a difference, too, so we wrote cards and letters for the 9/11 Tribute Museum telling families that lost loved ones on 9/11 that we have not forgotten and are thinking of them. The school also collected dollar donations from students for the charity Broadway Cares.

That's when we held another bake sale to raise even more money for Broadway Cares. The Sweet Treat Girls were at it again, making brownies, cupcakes, cookies, pretzels, strawberries and candies! It's not only fun to make a difference, but when you do something you enjoy and do it with your friends, that makes it even better.

Making a difference makes us happy because it helps others that don't have as much as we do. The experiences we've had make us feel proud that our hard work was able to make a difference. We plan to have more bake sales, and through The Sweet Treat Girls, we hope to encourage people to help others. Just because we are kids doesn't mean we can't make a difference in this big world. Doing something nice for someone can be fun to do, but it also means a lot. When we make a difference, we make other people's lives better, and we help out our community. It makes us feel good knowing that we are making an impact.

We hope other kids see the Sweet Treat Girls and get inspired to help others. We want to be a good example for our community and for other kids so that they can realize that they can do anything! Inspiring people is what making a difference is all about. We CAN make a difference!

Fiesta4Hope

Catherine Bagin and Rianna LeHane

Ten months after Hurricane Maria, I attended a school service trip to help with the devastation in Puerto Rico. Each day we were exposed to the various areas of need, including the reconstruction of houses, roads, businesses, and schools, along with the restoration of the beaches and rainforest.

On the second day of the trip, we planned on salvaging the remains of a family's fallen home so that pieces could be reused. When we arrived at the site, we learned this family was living on a cement slab while their eleven-month-old was in the hospital suffering from liver failure and malnutrition. The family survived off a "farm" in the backyard, which was a plot of soiled mud with ill animals crammed into tight pens. My friend Rianna and I were horrified to learn that Centro PASO, the nonprofit who took responsibility in connecting this family to broader means of aid, was running out of money. We knew there was so much more that needed to be done, and there would be no going back on the commitment we were about to make.

Less than a week after returning home, we created our fundraiser—the Fiesta4Hope Public Market. Not exactly sure where to start, we designed Fiesta4Hope's website, imagining a fun day of shopping, games, food, and live music. We compiled a list of potential vendors, containing local businesses that ranged from antique shops to boutiques. We pitched our mission, driving from town to town and explaining our cause. Broadening our target audience, we solicited stores that attracted different ages and genders and opened the event to garage sale tables. A local student band made their debut and provided the entertainment. Securing a food truck was our greatest obstacle, and we made over sixty calls before finding a deli excited to work with us.

We promoted the event through flyers, newspapers, and church bulletins, as well as on Facebook and Instagram. With over three hundred attendees, it was eye-opening to see how quickly the two-dollar entrance fees, vendor fees, and donations added up to eight thousand dollars, validating the overlooked mantra that "every little bit counts."

With the first year almost behind us and nearly fifteen thousand dollars to show for it, Rianna and I have stayed dedicated to helping Puerto Rico and Centro PASO. We have started Fiesta4Hope school chapters around the country, hoping to educate and empower teens while simultaneously raising money.

This summer we organized and chaperoned Fiesta4Hope's first service trip, taking twelve other girls to Puerto Rico to work with Centro PASO and provide aid to the still suffering town of Aibonito. We have also recently registered with New York State as a 501(c)3 trust, making Fiesta4Hope an official nonprofit organization. Our mission in helping the people of Puerto Rico rebuild their beautiful island home and restore their lives is humbling. We know how fortunate we are to live the life that we do and how fulfilling it is to bring joy and hope to people in need.

Milk Money for Tanzania

Isabella Benedetto

Hello, person who is reading this essay! Nice to meet you! My name is Isabella Benedetto. I am thirteen years old and in seventh grade. I go to Our Lady of Mercy Catholic Academy. My story isn't just about me, though; it's about my entire school and how we made a difference.

One day during our Social Studies class, our teacher began telling us about a place called Tanzania and a charity called Milk Money. We learned that Tanzania is a country in Africa. This country, while beautiful, is facing many financial problems. Schools there don't have enough money to provide meals for students. For some kids, this is their only meal, and so many kids become malnourished. Milk Money works with farmers to produce milk and package it for school kids.

To support this Milk Money fundraiser, my class and many others did various things with different teachers. We made Google Slides to show statistics (things like population shown in graphs) for Math, a landforms slide (grasslands, plains) for Science, and a religion slide (Christianity, nonreligious, etc.) for religion class. Each of our groups then presented these slides for the younger grades. My group presented our findings to the fourth-graders, and they really liked it.

In our presentation we explained why milk is so important. Milk is important because it contains protein, vitamins, and minerals such as calcium. All of these things help us grow, become strong, and fight off diseases.

Now we get to the best part: the actual fundraiser! To support Milk

Money, each class had to make a Tanzania/Milk Money jar. One class painted the Tanzania flag on their jar. My class, though, definitely had the best jar (totally not being biased). Our jar had printed pictures of a cow and milk cartoons on it! It also looks like a cow with black-and-white splotches. The point of these jars is for students at my school to donate money to Milk Money. For the amount of money you donate, you get a certain number of little flyers stating that you donated. I, of course, donated, but my friends donated so much more. My friends Chris and Daniel together donated over $200 just by themselves.

We all love this fundraiser and continue to donate every day! It's shown us that together we can make a difference in faraway places, as well as right here in the way we work together at school.

Three Wishes

Ruby Kate Chitsey

Three Wishes for Ruby's Residents is a project I started to serve residents in America's nursing homes. My project started small, at a nursing home in Arkansas where my mom works. One of the residents, Pearl, lost her dog because she only received forty dollars a month to spend on herself and her dog. When I saw that, I decided to start a local fundraiser to help people like her. I would ask each resident to tell me three wishes I could bring them. They always asked for simple items like snacks, clothes that fit, or pet food. I wrote them all in a journal, and I brought back their wishes.

As time went by, I kept asking questions, and I learned that there

were almost a million people like Pearl in America with about a forty-dollar allowance per month. The residents use this money to cover *a lot* of expenses, such as haircuts, pet food, new clothes, grocery items, cell phone service, and cable TV. They sometimes choose between keeping their cable TV on or buying themselves better shoes.

Once I learned how huge this problem was, I decided to create a larger, national fundraiser to help all the nursing home residents I could. I have now raised over $250,000 for my cause. Three Wishes for Ruby's Residents became a nonprofit in February 2019, and I am the CEO. We are starting Three Wishes chapters in several states so we can help people like Pearl all over the country. Nursing home residents shouldn't have to go without new clothes, haircuts, better shoes, or small things that make people happy on the inside, and Three Wishes makes sure they don't. I love giving them their favorite snacks and teaching others in different states to do the same.

We want to save their pets too. Three Wishes provides tons of pet food to help the residents feed their pets so they don't have to give them up. We adopted a cat for one nursing home. We've also added TVs for many residents who didn't even have one to watch. We make sure they have books that are actually readable and enjoyable. We've given every resident a new pillow. We also have fast-food days where we bring in a fast-food meal for every resident for lunch that day—like a Happy Meal.

My goal is making nursing home people smile again all over the country. That's huge because not too many people do anything for the nursing homes, especially the poor nursing homes, but I am determined to change that forever.

Giving the Gift of Music

Karl Kilb

My Eagle Scout project, "Let's Band Together," combined my love of music and my commitment to community service. The project involved collecting, refurbishing, and donating more than one hundred instruments to New York City Public Schools that needed the instruments to establish and support music programs. The instruments included keyboards, electric and acoustic guitars, violins, violas, clarinets, trumpets, flutes, cellos, and saxophones.

As a music major at LaGuardia High School of Music & Art and Performing Arts in New York City, I feel very fortunate that I get to do what I love every day. Instead of being considered an extracurricular activity, my music education is a core part of my overall high school education. In addition to taking a standard curriculum, I play piano and clarinet and take classes in music theory, music history, and performance.

Unfortunately, arts programs are usually the first thing to go when school budgets are cut. I wanted to make a difference in the lives of other students by giving them a chance to experience music and see if they could make a connection the way I have. Music has been a big part of my life from an early age. I started playing the piano at the age of five, and the clarinet when I turned eight.

One of the biggest challenges I faced during my project was finding a way to move a donated baby grand piano from a private house in Brooklyn to a grammar school in New York City's Lower East Side. With the help of my family and fellow scouts, I made and sold chocolates in the shape of musical instruments at churches and schools to raise funds to refurbish the used instruments. I was able

to raise enough money to arrange for the piano to be moved to the grammar school, and it became the centerpiece of their new music program.

The principal held a special assembly the day the piano and other instruments were delivered, and I was invited to speak to the students and play the donated piano. I was overwhelmed by their gratitude and enthusiasm for the gift of music.

This project is impacting thousands of students at six public schools, and it will continue to benefit thousands of more students in the future. The project took months to complete, but it has exceeded my expectations.

My best memories of the many hours devoted to the project were the warm and sometimes emotional reactions I received from students and teachers who benefited from the instrument drive. I also enjoyed doing media coverage for my project, including a "live" appearance on WNYW-TV Channel 5 in New York with anchorman Ernie Anastos and other interviews.

Studies show that playing an instrument can stimulate the brain and help improve focus, concentration, and productivity. Music opened up a whole new world for me and gave me a creative outlet that I hope to turn into a career as a music producer and composer. I also hope to have a nonprofit Music Foundation in the future that is dedicated to music programs in schools.

The Book That Started It All

Alivia Parks

Have you ever had a book that meant so much to you that you read it over and over again? Well, I sure have, and that book is *Loukoumi's Gift.*

The reason I love this book so much is that it has a special place in my heart. Even though I got the book when I was only one, my mom and dad read the book to me every day because I met the author and fell in love with the Loukoumi mascot.

Photo Credit: St. Jude Children's Research Hospital

And that's when it all started. I got the book when I was in St. Jude Children's Research Hospital because I had bilateral retinoblastoma, which is a cancer of the retinas in both eyes.

I was in the hospital for more than four months. It was the hardest time of my life, and that Loukoumi book made me calm though my chemo treatments.

The next year Nick Katsoris (the author) sent me my second-favorite book, *Loukoumi's Good Deeds*. He even signed it for me and wrote "Do something nice!"

I found out that he was giving money from his books to St. Jude, and that made me want to be kind to everybody. St. Jude started calling me their little mascot. After that I wanted to give money to St. Jude, the people who saved my life.

That year I did my first two fundraisers for St. Jude, and my family and I have not stopped since—because a child with cancer deserves more! We have raised a lot of money for St. Jude, and the Loukoumi books inspire me to do more for everyone!

They inspire me because, as *Loukoumi's Gift* says:

> A gift is a thought your heart creates,
> and need not cost a penny.
> A gift can be anything that you wish,
> made for one or many.
> A thoughtful act, a handmade card,
> a delicious cookie or cake;
> the perfect gift is straight from the
> heart, whatever it is you make."

These sayings make me want to give to others, cheer people up, help friends when they need help, and listen when they are going through hard times. Even though I'm only ten years old, that doesn't stop me from giving to others.

Hopefully you have been inspired by something in your life to help others and do "good deeds." It doesn't take much to change a person's day—it can start with a smile on your face!

Read & Write Up a Storm!

Teagan Ralph

Read and Write Up a Storm was my idea with a little help from my friends and family. It is crazy how this idea started from watching our TV and has expanded to tons of parents and children who either helped make a difference or were someone who needed help. I've been able to help lots of kids in Texas have books and notebooks so they can continue to improve their reading and writing.

It was a warm autumn day in 2017 when I walked into my mother's room and saw such a terrible mess on TV, the aftermath of

Hurricane Harvey. I saw a boy throwing away his clothes and toys. Then I saw him throwing away his books and notebooks. I thought, *That's not right—every kid should have the chance to read and write. Don't our teachers tell us to read and write up a storm so that we can get better?* A light bulb went on in my head. I started to think that we should start an organization called Read & Write Up a Storm.

The next day when I went to school, I talked to my principal and told her about my idea to send books to Texas. She said it was a great idea for our school! A week later two friends and I gave a presentation and asked for kids to donate books and notebooks. We collected over two hundred books and notebooks and sent them to a friend of my dad's in Texas who said he could help find a school that needed them. I thought that was the end of the story . . .

A few months later my dad got a call from his friend in Texas. His friend is in a union and he said that he had given a speech at the state union meeting and used my story. He shared that one girl from the smallest state in the nation came up with a way to help. After the speech people donated more books and notebooks—*a lot more* books and notebooks. In all there were over 20,000 books donated! And this wasn't the end of the story . . .

One morning while watching TV, I saw that another storm had passed through Puerto Rico and destroyed everything. I realized that the Read & Write Up a Storm story was not over. I was proud of all we did to help, but I realized that there was still a lot more work to be done. We are still gathering more books to send to Puerto Rico. Hopefully we can help more kids be able to Read & Write Up a Storm!

A New Perspective

Arietta Xylas

My name is Arietta Xylas and I am fourteen years old. My family and I first discovered the Loukoumi Foundation when Mr. Katsoris visited my school to read some of his books. I was in the fourth grade, and ever since then the Loukoumi Foundation has continued to inspire me to make a change in our world.

I've always liked to read, and I can't imagine not being able to have access to books. My mom and I decided that we would donate as many books as we could to a school in Lesotho, Southern Africa. The whole project showed me how much people can really do together just by asking for help. We printed flyers for every kid in my school. It was really surreal for a fourth-grader because people began handing me books left and right to contribute. I often would come home from school with two full bags of books, which we would then need to count, sort, and eliminate any that were in bad shape or inappropriate. People also donated cash to buy books. Eventually we collected over one thousand books for the library.

Participating in the African Library Project opened my eyes to a whole new world of possibility for how I could help others. If I was able to help a whole school in Africa by providing them a library, imagine all the other things I would be able to do with the same determination.

From that point on, my mom and I try to do at least one project each year. One year we did a coat drive as a way to help people who could not afford warm coats to get through the winter. This year we did a canned food drive in an attempt to supply people in need with

food for Thanksgiving. In addition to setting up a stand to collect canned goods, I stayed after school to sell baked goods in order to raise money for the cause. The weekend after the money and food was collected, we traveled all around New York delivering turkeys, canned food, and bread to needy families. It was an eye-opening experience to see people's living conditions, and I was sad I could not help everyone.

But that's the beauty of the Loukoumi Foundation: there are so many people doing so many wonderful things that you're never short of an idea of how to help. Recently the Loukoumi Foundation took as many kids as they could on a trip to clean up a nature park. It was really beautiful to see so many different kinds of people all working together to make a difference. Even though we were just raking leaves and donating pet supplies, I felt like we were doing something good together.

Being a part of the Loukoumi Foundation has completely changed my perspective on the world. This foundation brings people with the same goals together to form something truly unique and special, and I'm glad to say I've been able to make a difference.

Be an Inspiration

Sheyla Zarate

What does the word *inspiring* mean to you? To me it means encouraging someone to do something good. When I think of a time when I inspired someone, I think of an older woman named Lorraine.

It all started twelve years ago. Lorraine came to my mom's hair salon to get her hair done. As she and my mom talked, Lorraine mentioned that her niece had just had a baby boy, but because her family lived so far away, she was not able to visit the baby. My mom told her, "Well, I am having a baby in a couple weeks, and you are welcome to come to the hospital to visit us." So they exchanged phone numbers, and sure enough, a couple of weeks later my mom called Lorraine, and she came to the hospital as quickly as she could.

I've inspired Lorraine from the moment I was born. People always say that I keep her more active and younger, but I think that is just who she is. She actually fed me my first bottle because my mom had a cesarean section and was too sore, and my dad was at home taking care of my other sisters. She is just a family friend, but I think of Lorraine like a grandmother.

As I grew up, I became even closer to her. When I was little, I would go to my mom's salon, and Lorraine would be there to feed me and carry me around. I feel like I have made a huge difference in her life. I think I have made her happier, livelier, and just a better person.

Lorraine has also inspired me and made me a better person. She helps me to do better in school and encourages me to always believe in myself. She helps me with my homework and school projects. She also is very kind; when she sees a homeless person or a person in need, she helps them. I am so grateful for her!

Lorraine is an amazing person. I am so happy she met my mom because she has inspired me, and I've been able to inspire her too. I hope God blesses her with many more years of life.

EVERYONE IS DIFFERENT, YET WE'RE REALLY ALL THE SAME

"Everyone is different, yet we're really all the same.
I shouldn't make fun of someone, especially their name.
I shouldn't be a bully because it really isn't cool.
We should be accepting of others, that's the golden rule!"

Loukoumi and the Schoolyard Bully
NARRATED BY NIA VARDALOS AND MORGAN FREEMAN

Never Give Up

Emily Garcia

Whenever I think of an inspiring moment in my life, I think about the time when I didn't understand a math problem in third grade, and my teacher, Mrs. Barresi, inspired me. It all started off at math time. We were learning about division and multiplication. In my opinion, I personally thought that division was too hard to learn in third grade. I thought I would never be capable of understanding the concept of multiplication and division. I kept trying and trying, but I couldn't seem to get it at all.

I ended up crying because I felt like I wasn't smart enough. I was sad because all my friends seemed to understand it. I also didn't want to tell my teacher that I didn't understand because I would have been embarrassed.

Once I started crying, though, I caught Mrs. Barresi's attention, and she walked over to my desk. She told me, "Emily, it is OK! Life has multiple challenges waiting for you. Don't ever give up, and always keep trying as hard as you can." Her words inspired me because she taught me that I shouldn't give up in any hard situation I may have to go through. She also taught me how to pick myself up. This was a moment I won't forget.

Overall, hearing my third-grade teacher telling me not to give up inspired me. Now, every time something gets rough, I always pick myself up and keep trying. Whether it's a school subject like multiplication and division or something challenging I'll encounter outside of school, I now know I can keep trying and never give up. I hope to inspire others the way Mrs. Barresi inspired me!

Dance to Make a Difference

Kayleigh Geagan

I love to dance. It is my favorite thing to do. I am a dancer, but it took a lot of hard work and time to become one.

When I was little, my mom told me stories about when she was young. She had been a dancer, and I loved listening to stories about the dance competitions she went to, the classes she took, and all the hard work and passion she put into dancing. She inspired me, and I decided that I wanted to be a dancer too.

My mom signed me up for dance classes right away, at the same place she had taken dance lessons: her mother's dance studio, Miss

Andrea's Dance Studio. When I was three, I went to my first dance recital! I was nervous, but I did great! I knew it wouldn't be my last performance.

I admired famous ballerinas like Misty Copeland. I did many more recitals and shows, and I loved it! But in kindergarten, I realized that I was very short for my age. Most of the other kids were way taller than me, and it made me feel out of place. One kid even thought that was a reason to tease me. When that mean kid found out that I wanted to be a dancer, he laughed even harder. He said I was too short to be a dancer and told me my dreams would never come true. That wasn't the only reason he bullied me. He made fun of my backpack, my drawings—even the way I talked! But I never thought he was right. Once he said a horrible word on the bus ride home that made me cry! It was awful, and I knew it had to stop.

I taught myself to shut out all the insults and think about the day when I would prove to that bully that I could be a dancer. When I was six, I performed in my first dance competition. I was so nervous that I forgot my dance midway through my performance. I invented my own steps and kept going. I was upset afterward, but my mom and my dance teacher, Miss Stephanie, said I did what a smart dancer would do. The judges didn't even realize that I forgot my dance, and I won my category! I kept going to dance competitions, and the bullying kept going on too—all the way up to second grade. But I never stopped doing what *I loved.*

I joined an anti-bullying Kindness Club at school, and we were invited to speak at our school assembly about how hurtful bullying can be. After that, the mean boy stopped bullying me and never tried to make me feel sad again. That didn't change my confidence level or how I felt about myself, though, because I had been confident all along in spite of how he acted.

So, if you ever feel like you're not right for something or like you don't belong, just keep doing what you love. If it makes you happy, then do it! It doesn't matter what mean people think about you! Just be yourself.

Rainbow-Colored Ponies

Adriana Hansen

My story began when I was four years old and was put into foster care. In just over seven months, I was moved into three different homes before I found my forever family. It was a scary time for me, and I didn't know what was happening.

Before my adoption was final, my mom talked with me about helping other kids who are still in foster care and haven't found their forever families yet. I told her that I thought the kids would love to have stuffed ponies. When my mom asked me what color ponies, I told her they should be rainbow-colored. That night a story came to my mom, and she shared it with me. It was about a little girl who had some mixed-up feelings from missing someone that she loved. The little girl was hugging her stuffed pony when the pony came alive, turned rainbow-colored, and gave the girl three messages to help her through her feelings. That story turned into a children's book. My mom and I decided that we wanted to donate the books and ponies to kids in foster care.

My goal is to give away as many books and ponies as we can to as many children as we can. So far, we have given away over three hundred ponies and books, and we plan to continue raising money to purchase more. The kids can relate to the book because it helps them see how they don't have to keep all the sad and angry feelings inside. Those feelings are normal, and it's OK to feel them, but then they have the power to let them go. It also shows kids how they can stay connected to the ones they are missing through invisible heart strings. The stuffed ponies give the kids something tangible they can

relate to. The ponies cheer the kids up, and it helps them feel safe and loved. Doing this makes me feel happy, too, because I know what it feels like to be lonely, sad, and scared.

In November 2018 I started a GoFundMe campaign and was picked to be the GoFundMe Kid Hero for the month of March! As part of my fundraiser, I also wanted to help send a group of foster care kids through the local equine-assisted psychotherapy program. We have raised over twenty-thousand dollars, and that is helping us give away many more books and ponies and also sponsor a few kids to attend this amazing program. My mom and dad are helping me turn this into a nonprofit so I can continue to give and make a difference in the world!

Believing in a Beggar

Darren Ke

My mom and dad own a restaurant in the Bronx, New York. They are busy most of the day, especially during lunchtime. They are normally very nice to all of their customers, but on certain days when it is very busy, they are usually not lenient toward people asking for food or other things. I remember a certain beggar that said he was homeless, but nobody believed him. After all, he had pretty nice sneakers and was wearing nice clothes. He kept pleading for food, saying he didn't have much to eat these days. My parents were reluctant to give food to him, but they eventually did when he kept pleading for help.

A few months passed without him coming to the restaurant. One day, my parents and I decided to travel to Manhattan to shop for some new school apparel. While we were walking to a clothing shop, there he was, the beggar that had come to our store! He apparently hoped he could make more money begging in Manhattan than in the Bronx. However, we saw people relentlessly making fun of him and mocking him. Instead of his previous appearance back in the Bronx, he now looked sad and disheveled, with a ripped shirt, sandals with ripped soles, ragged pants, and a dirty face, and a cup to collect change. The cup only had about two dollars' worth of change in it.

The homeless person recognized my parents and waved at them, trying to get their attention. My parents simply looked the other way, but I recognized him immediately. I waved to him, and he smiled at me. Without my parents seeing, I dropped a five-dollar bill into his cup. He looked at me with the most sincere and grateful look in his eyes; I will never forget it. On my way back to the Bronx, I thought about him and wanted to try to find a way to help him.

A year passed, and now I was eight years old. One day I went to the supermarket to get some groceries, and I saw the same homeless person in ragged clothes, with a dirtied face, and a cup that was about to fall apart. I immediately gave him some money again. I bought my groceries, and when I came outside, he asked if I knew of any jobs nearby. I said, "Maybe," and I ran home to ask my parents if they would hire another person

in their restaurant. My parents said yes, but the person would only get minimum wage. I relayed this to the homeless person, and he jumped for joy.

This homeless man worked at my parents' restaurant for two years. By then he had saved enough money to buy a house for his family. To this day, my parents still don't remember that he was the beggar they gave food to. I am happy that I was able to make a difference in the life of someone, and I look forward to helping more people in the future.

Arthritis Doesn't Define Me

Irene Maris

Imagine that you wake up one day and can't move any of your joints. You can't walk, run, write, draw, or do anything else you do on a daily basis.

That's what happened to me. I'm fifteen years old, and when I was only sixteen months old, I was diagnosed with juvenile rheumatoid arthritis. This type of arthritis attacks more than five joints. I was not able to walk, crawl, or do other things that kids did at that age. My mom took me to the doctor to find out what was wrong, and the news that I had arthritis was a shock to my family. My family didn't know that kids could get arthritis too.

The rheumatologist who we found to take care of me was a very

nice doctor, and she advised my mom that I needed to start taking medication and begin physical and occupational therapy so my joints could work again. My mom did what the doctor told her right away. She told me she remembered crying and asking my physical therapist if I would be able to walk again.

Having to deal with an autoimmune disease at such a young age was difficult. I had bad days, and I had good days. There were days that I didn't want to take my medication. I couldn't understand why I had to suffer and go through this.

The pain affected me physically, but it also affected the way I was thinking. I was worried that others would laugh and make fun of me if they found out what I was suffering from. I felt sad when I saw everyone else enjoying what they were doing, while I was struggling to do the everyday tasks we take for granted.

One day my mother and myself tried to join the walk in the city for the Arthritis Foundation, but due to other walks that were happening the same day and a lot of traffic, we never made it. We both were very upset, but we didn't give up. We started a fundraiser at our church and raised some money for the foundation, and that made me very happy.

Every year since then, we've participated in the walk to cure arthritis, and we hold several fundraisers annually. I want to make a difference, bring awareness, help others, and hopefully help doctors to find a cure one day. We formed a team called Team Irene. For about six years now we have raised over $30,000 for the Arthritis Foundation. I have been nominated two times to be the honoree for the Foundation, and I have received a few awards for my hard work!

Even though I still suffer from arthritis today, with the help of my doctors and medications, I'm able to enjoy most of the things I like, including basketball!

I will not allow arthritis to define me!

I will try my best to help others, and I would like to become a pediatric rheumatologist to help the 300,000 kids that suffer from this disease.

Kind Girls Rule!

Nicole Nelson

I'm eight years old, and I love singing, dancing, gymnastics, and modeling. Sometimes I walk the runway for children's designers in New York's Fashion Weeks, which are held in February and September, and someone challenged me to be more than just a "fashion model" and instead be a "role model." Challenge accepted! In response, I created a social media charitable platform, "Kind Girls Rule the World" (KGRTW) to promote awareness, inclusion, and giving back to the autism and epilepsy communities.

Why are these two causes so important to me? Because I have an older brother, Jordon, who is twenty-one years old and was diagnosed with ASD (Autism Spectrum Disorder) when he was four. He experienced his first seizure and was diagnosed with epilepsy when he was seventeen years old. As his little sister, I am his loudest and biggest advocate and supporter!

Some days, I struggle to understand the "what" and "why" of autism and epilepsy, so I've made it my goal to learn as much as I can, to share as much as I learn, and to give back to these amazingly special people and communities through volunteerism and fundraising. Kind Girls Rule the World is my answer to the "why."

My brother's seizures aren't always controlled with medication, and our family is in the process of trying a new seizure medication to see if it will work better. Right now, he's taking two medications, but hopefully soon he'll just be on the one new medication. For many people who have epilepsy, the excessive cost of seizure medications each month is one of the biggest problems they face. I want to help pay it forward! On

January 21, 2019, KGRTW kicked off its first fundraiser to benefit the Epilepsy Foundation of Delaware Yara's Fund. This foundation supports an emergency medication program to provide assistance to individuals with epilepsy who struggle to pay for their medication.

To raise money for Yara's Fund, I'm collecting gently worn, used, or new shoes, and money is raised based on the number of shoes collected. My goal is one hundred bags of shoes collected (approximately 2,500 pairs or twenty-five pairs of shoes per bag). I chose a shoe drive because it's a no-cost fundraiser and simply involves cleaning out your closets. All types, sizes, and styles of shoes are accepted. Donating these shoes means that they won't sit in landfills; instead they are given to micro-entrepreneurs in developing countries, such as Haiti, who create jobs by repurposing and reselling the shoes.

Launching the shoe drive has been an amazing experience! It's allowed me to go out into my community to meet new people, spread awareness, and create partnerships who support my fundraiser. I'm excited and proud to say that three of the Delaware YMCAs, the Police Athletic League (PAL) of Delaware, and The Blue Coats/76ers Fieldhouse are KGRTW's strongest supporters.

Together we can make a difference, and I can't wait to see what the future holds!

Woya Woya Nu Koko (Come Eat Your Porridge)

Panayiotis "Niko" Papaioannou

In July 2018, I learned how to sing. I also learned to see the best in people and to connect with everyone around me. I learned all that and more across the Atlantic Ocean, in a humble country named Ghana. People were happy there. They loved their lives and took nothing for granted.

The summer between my ninth and tenth grade, I participated in a volunteer program called "Promoting Children's Rights and Education" in Legon, Ghana. On our first day of service, as the bus pulled up outside the Cristah International School, my heart began to melt as I heard the sound of little children singing. Inside, thirty beautiful little kids stormed me, cheering and hugging. They all spoke English remarkably well. I also learned a lot about their native language, Twi, during my time volunteering at the school.

I helped the students with English and I also taught them Math and Religion. The religion class was my favorite because the whole class stood up and recited prayers and sang beautiful passages. I taught the students a song I learned from my Boy Scout camp called "Rise and Shine." They all enjoyed it very much and recited it every day before class started.

One day I pulled out my notebook. All of the children quickly surrounded me, asking for a piece of paper. I gave everyone in the class one piece of paper. However, after a couple of minutes, one of the students said he lost his. Soon everyone else in the class was asking for more paper. I finally realized that they were hiding the papers under their seats, saying they lost it, and asking for more. This

made me see how much we take for granted in the U.S.—little things like pencils and paper.

One event sums up my experience in Ghana. During an afternoon culture class, the volunteers learned a song called "Woya Woya Nu Koko," which translates to "Come to Eat Your Porridge."

This song originated many years ago to signify a sense of unity among the community, as the tradition in Ghana was for everyone in the town to share a communal bowl of porridge.

After learning this simple, three-line song, I would sing it everywhere I went. One time I was at the farmer's market with one of my friends, looking for some fresh mango. We decided to start singing the song out loud to see who would recognize it. Much to our surprise, the ladies at the vendor next to us began singing with us. Soon half the market was singing along with us. It was undoubtedly one of the purest and happiest moments of my life. Total strangers, from opposite sides of the world, opposite cultures, and opposite backgrounds, coming together and uniting over one simple song! It made me realize that everybody, no matter the culture, can always find common ground and be happy together. After all, we all eat from the same porridge bowl in the end.

Accepting Others

Lucy Skipper

The Loukoumi Make A Difference Foundation is really spectacular! The Loukoumi Foundation has collaborated with a bunch of groups and other foundations to inspire young kids, teens, and adults to change their community—and the world—to be a happier place. I am very grateful to be a part of it!

Eastchester, New York, is a very diverse community made up of many different cultures. I have friends who are Italian, Irish, Japanese, Greek, Armenian, Columbian, German, Indian, and Asian. I hear them speak their native language in their homes, and I share their different lunches with them in the cafeteria. Loukoumi teaches us to be accepting of all of our friends, even if they're not exactly like us.

One day I was riding the bus on the way home from school. I noticed a Japanese student who was in the second grade. From riding with him throughout the year, I knew that he was just learning English; it was not his native language. This particular day, his seat belt had fallen off his lap and he didn't notice. A third-grader yelled at him to put his seat belt back on, but the second-grader didn't understand him because he still mostly spoke only Japanese. He started crying, but the third-grader kept yelling at him.

When the bus stopped, I jumped up and asked the Japanese boy if he was OK, and I started to help him with his seat belt. While I was buckling it, his open backpack slipped off the seat, and everything fell out onto the bus floor! I quickly helped him gather all of his belongings, and I kept telling him that it was OK. I sat with him for the rest of the bus ride, and I stayed with him until his mom came to meet him at the bus stop. I hoped he would feel better, and the next day when I saw him, he gave me a big smile! I was very happy for him, and I was glad I did what I did!

I try to practice what Loukoumi teaches every day. I hope that Loukoumi continues to grow throughout the United States and the whole world!

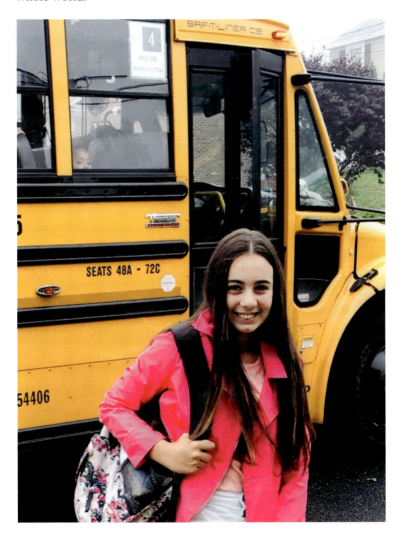

A Call to Service

Will Tinson

Serving others has always been important to me, and I have taken advantage of opportunities to help people whenever I can. Perhaps my most significant effort was in working with Food Allergy Research and Education, or FARE. This organization leads educational outreach, research initiatives, and advocacy programs.

Over five million children in the United States live with food allergies, and an additional ten million adults have food allergies as well. While I personally do not have any food allergies, many of the people closest to me do, especially my older brother. Growing up with a sibling that has severe milk allergies has raised my awareness of this epidemic. As a family, we have been involved with FARE for as long as I can remember. My brother became a Teen Ambassador for the national organization, and we all participate annually in their Food Allergy Heroes Walk, among other service projects.

When I was in the sixth grade, I was offered the chance to compete against the rest of my middle school to pitch a charity and fundraising campaign as part of our Student Leadership Service Learning Initiative, or SL2. When I thought about the importance of what FARE stands for, it was the obvious choice. I worked tirelessly to perfect my presentation using a three-stage process, and I ended up winning.

I spent the rest of the year planning my campaign before its launch in early seventh grade. October is the month of the FARE walk, so that determined my time frame. I organized a school team that raised well over two thousand dollars for FARE. Then I held a bake sale consisting of all allergen-friendly food items, and I hosted a table at the Loukoumi Make A Difference Day event to raise additional funding for this noble cause. In all, I raised approximately five thousand dollars, which included a matched donation from an anonymous donor. In order to raise awareness at school, I organized different activities for each grade level to participate in over the course of the month, and I presented updates regularly at school assemblies. This year, I went back to the Loukoumi Make A Difference Day event to help sustain this effort.

I valued this experience to help those I love and others like them, so I decided to launch a new initiative to help even more people. This time, I was moved by the constant stories of victims from natural disasters. At the end of last year, I was once again given the chance to represent a charity of my choice. I am now supporting Save the Children in their Hurricane Maria Relief Fund in response to last year's tragedy. My work with FARE and Save the Children reflect how important the call to service has become in my life.

KINDNESS

"The secret to happiness is doing things for others;
looking out for friends, our sisters, and our brothers.
A little bit of kindness goes a long, long way,
and then our happiness is here to stay!"

Loukoumi in the Basket

NARRATED BY NANCY O'DELL

Sweet Dreams for Homeless Children

Julia Arditi and Malia Hernandez

Project Night Night is a nonprofit organization that helps children under twelve years old across the United States who are living in shelters. Its goal is to make the children feel safe and secure in a new and unfamiliar environment by providing "Night Night Packages." These packages consist of an age-appropriate book, a stuffed animal, and a blanket packaged in a tote. Working with Project Night Night has inspired us to educate others about the importance of making a difference and inspire others to make a difference too.

We learned about Project Night Night while participating in a service-learning project at The Chapel School. The project required participants to choose a charity and make a presentation to the board and school administrators. The winner would be able to have our school support an organization of our choice through one month of events.

We chose Project Night Night, an organization now very close to our hearts. We knew we could help this charity, and even if we did not raise a lot of money, it would still matter, especially to the children who benefited from our donations. Throughout October 2018 we organized events, collected offerings, and educated students and faculty at our school about Project Night Night. Some of the fundraising events we held included a non-uniform day and a movie night, where over forty attendees were able to learn more about the work we were doing for Project Night Night.

We also held service-learning opportunities for students at our school, which included reading books to preschoolers and helping to package one hundred Night Night Packages. Many children also learned about our project during Make A Difference Day at our school. Throughout the various weeks of planning, educating, and service, we have become inspired to keep doing service for the different people and children who will benefit from it. We will forever remember the feeling of joy we got from seeing smiling faces packaging Night Night Packages or when we had opportunities to talk about Project Night Night.

Helping others is always inspiring not only for yourself, but for your community as well. Whether it's by giving donations, volunteering, or hosting events such as 5Ks, there are so many ways to support an organization that is important to you. One of our goals while working with Project Night Night was to educate children and adults about our cause. We hope that when people see the work that we have done, they will become inspired to make a difference themselves.

We put a lot of work, time, and effort into our project, and it really paid off. Throughout the course of our project, we inspired others through our actions and events, and we were inspired by how much people helped us. We are both very grateful for getting the opportunity to make a difference, and we will always hold Project Night Night and the Loukoumi Foundation close to our hearts.

The International Day of Happiness

Danielle Gordon

What is the International Day of Happiness? It's a day to be happy, of course!

A few years ago, my mom told me she read an article that Pharrell Williams was turning his song "Happy" into a children's book series. I was in second grade at the time, and my mom and I use to write books for fun. I thought, *Who better to write a children's book than a child?* I asked my mom if I could write to Pharrell and ask him if I could help him write his books. What happened next would change my life, and hopefully the lives of everyone I know.

Long story short, we wrote to Pharrell, and he wrote back! He gave my mom an address where I could send my letter. My mom said we needed to learn everything we could possibly learn about Pharrell Williams in case we got to meet him. We learned that on June 28, 2013, the United Nations, along with Pharrell Williams, established March 20 as International Day of Happiness. Pharrell stated: "It is your birthright to be happy."

I asked my school principal, Mrs. DeLuca, if our school, Old Mill Road Elementary School, could celebrate the International Day of Happiness. She said yes, and the rest, as they say, is history.

Every year my school celebrates International Day of Happiness on March 20th. We have learned all ten components that make up "Happy Day," and we do something for each of the ten components. It's a pretty BIG deal at my school. We even shared it with our sister schools and our component schools; now we all celebrate on March 20th.

We learn to love ourselves for being unique. "There's no better you

than the YOU that you are." We all sing songs of happiness at an assembly. We eat healthy snacks, exercise, and create artwork featuring quotes such as "We are each unique and beautiful, but together we are a masterpiece." On the many posters with inspirational and positive messages, my mom paints the lyrics to the song "Happy," and we hang those posters all over the school. The song is playing on the loud speaker as all of us enter the school that day.

One of everyone's favorite activities on this day is to share compliments. I wanted everyone in the school to be able to tell someone else something positive about them. We can all find the good about ourselves by looking at ourselves through someone else's eyes. I now have four years' worth of collected compliments, and it makes my heart happy to read them from time to time.

On Happy Day we also raise money for a charity. I have developed what I intend to be a lifelong relationship with one of the charities, the Loukoumi Make A Difference Foundation. One year we participated in a fun run/5K run fundraiser. The school had read all the Loukoumi books, and Nick Katsoris, the foundation's founder and the author of the books, spoke at our assembly. All the registration fees raised were donated to the Loukoumi Foundation to spread the message of doing good deeds instead of being a bully.

My hope is that we can all learn to "be happy with ourselves" so no one bullies anyone else. I'll always remember one poster that read: "Be so happy that when others look at you, they become happy too."

And Happy Day does not have to be limited to March 20!

A Surprise for Mom

Jayda S. Payne

My inspiring story starts on a not-so-normal Monday in the month of June 2018. The weekend before, my mom had one of her excruciating headaches, but she continued to be a supermom doing laundry, cooking, homework, and just being a mom. My three-year-old brother and I were waiting for her to pick us up after school as usual. Instead, my dad picked us up. When we got into the car, I asked, "Where is Mom?" He replied, "She's in the hospital."

When I asked why, he told me that the doctors didn't know yet. We went through two days without her. On the second day in the hospital, she was diagnosed with Transient Ischemic Attack (TIA). Google explains this as a "weakness, or loss of function, on one side of the body."

Soon everyone in my fourth-grade class knew. My closest friends knew that if something bad happened, it would affect me badly. They were always there for me. Then I came up with the most brilliant idea to make my mom feel better. I did what I normally did best: make "feel better" cards. My classmates saw me cutting paper and drawing. I could see they wanted to question me, but they kept quiet. (Of course, I did this early in the morning before class started.) At recess, I asked my teacher to sign the card, and then I asked everyone in my class to sign the card, and they did. My teacher let me go around the school and ask other students and teachers to sign the card too.

Now came the big surprise I planned for my mom. After school, I put the card in her bedroom and FaceTimed my mom on my dad's phone. She said she was getting better already. I told her that I had a present for her. She wanted to know what it was, but I told her it was a surprise. I was waiting for the day when she would finally come home.

In the meantime, I had to have everything planned perfectly. That meant dishes must be washed, floors had to be cleaned, beds needed to be made up, and dirty clothes washed and put away. Our house was very busy the day before my mom came home!

My mom spent five days in the hospital recovering from her sickness, and when she finally came home, I ran to her and hugged her. I showed her all that I had done. I showed her the card. She hugged me and opened it. She said, "This is the nicest thing in the world," and started to cry. She also told me that I was the best daughter in the world. That is exactly how I felt!

My mother had to do some physical therapy to help with her balance and grip, but thank God that she was given back to us!

We're Out to Change Our World

K-Kids at PS 205

We are the K-Kids at PS 205, a community service club that is part of Kiwanis International. Our club is a student-led club of kids who are eager to make a difference.

Fordham University has sponsored the club since 2014 and we have developed a great relationship with the Fordham University-Key Club, especially with Thomas and Dr. Rosemary DeJulio, Former Kiwanis International President and First Lady.

The K-Kids at PS 205 consist of fourth- and fifth-graders. As the fifth-graders graduate, the fourth-graders continue to lead the club.

Every year we embark on many projects, including a school-wide volunteer project.

This year we were motivated by the Fordham University Kiwanis Club President, Sister Anne-Marie Kirmse, to help a homeless organization called Socks in the City. When we learned about it, we were excited to get other students involved.

We participated in a web conference where we met Catherine Fernando, the founder of Socks in the City. We made flyers, and our president and vice president made announcements over the loudspeaker to encourage students and staff to get involved. As a community service-driven school, not only did students participate, but parents and staff also participated, and we were able to donate socks and a monetary contribution to Socks in the City.

Three years ago, the president of K-Kids had an idea to start a fundraising talent show. Each year, the money collected supports an organization and a need in the school. We were able to collect $355 for St. Jude Children's Research Hospital. The students also made "Caring Cards" for patients at the hospital. The talent show has remained an end of the year celebration that students, parents, and staff all look forward to.

This year some of us also assisted in the Conversational English Club, which helps immigrant students learn conversational English skills. We also have developed a friendship with club members. One day, a fourth-grader was having a hard time translating for a student who spoke Arabic and he went to Google Translate to interpret the questions. Another fourth-grade student had a hard time explaining what a board game is, so he went to Google Images to look up visuals of board games. These students gave up their lunch period and took their role seriously.

Our advisor, Myrlene Michel, says that she is "always amazed at the leadership skills of the students. Every year, they come up with great volunteer opportunities. The students are always ready to serve. I am confident that these students are going to change the world!"

Frogs, Pen Pals, and Plastic Pollution

Justin Sather

I am eight years old, and I live in Los Angeles, California. I love to play sports, hang out with my friends, build things, and I really LOVE frogs! I would have never guessed that my love for frogs would turn into a passion for taking care of the planet.

It all started in kindergarten, when I learned that *frogs are disappearing*. Almost one-third of frog species are on the verge of extinction. I found out pollution, pesticides, and habitat destruction are the main causes for their decline. I also learned that frogs are indicator species. Frogs are telling us that the planet needs our help.

I became interested in recycling, but when I learned that trash can be transformed into other gadgets . . . it was like MAGIC! I discovered ways to keep trash out of landfills. I switched to reusable snack bags and gave lessons on composting. I learned how to recycle crayons, turn fishing line into bracelets, and transform plastic bags into doormats. Then I came across a little girl named Sammie who melts two hundred pounds of plastic bottle caps into a buddy bench that encourages kindness and new friendships.

That's when things got exciting!

In the summer of 2018, I wrote a letter to Sammie in Indiana to learn more about the buddy benches. I learned that a buddy bench is a place where students can go at recess when they are feeling lonely, upset, or want to make new friends. I was beyond excited about the concept, and that's when our weekly pen pal letter writing began. Within weeks, I decided I wanted to bring Sammie's Buddy Benches to California. I started collecting caps from my family, neighbors, classmates, the local

YMCA, Walgreens, and the Microsoft Theater. The Staples Center even collected caps for me at an Elton John concert. After six months of collecting, I reached the two hundred-pound goal!

I wanted to meet Sammie in person. After nine months of writing, my family decided that we could fly the 2,162 miles to Indiana for Spring Break. It was the most incredible trip ever. First, we stopped in Fort Wayne to meet Sammie and her family, and then we saw the first buddy bench Sammie made at her school. Then we drove five hours to Evansville, and I got to see my two hundred pounds of caps melted down for my school's bench. Turning trash into treasure is truly just like magic—it was a dream come true!

On Earth Day, I presented the buddy bench to my school. It was very exciting. That night I received a surprise message. It was from a twenty-two-year-old boy from Cameroon that was inspired by my work. He asked if I could help him turn his plastic trash into treasures all the way in Africa. I agreed to help him because I believe in the power of pen pals.

And I want to help our planet—all for my love of frogs!

Making a Difference at a Young Age

Tyler Stallings

I am the eight-year-old CEO of Kid Time Enterprises, LLC. The motto of Kid Time Enterprises is "Future Leaders Can Change the World, One Idea at a Time." I am located in Halethorpe, Maryland. Through Kid Time Enterprises, I have two volunteer projects. The first one is Give Back to Veterans. I spread kindness by raising awareness about helping veterans in the community. I help homeless veterans and elderly veterans to get back on their feet, but I also thank all veterans. My second is Tyler's #1000bookgiveaway. I have given away 11,000 free books so far.

I do my veteran project because veterans have served our country. I started it after I watched videos about veterans. Some videos were about their service, and others were about how many veterans were homeless. I took immediate action and told my mom that I wanted to help homeless veterans by building houses for them. My mom explained that it was not in our budget to build houses, but we could come up with something else.

After a few days, Mom and I co-founded Give Back to Veterans Day. I set a time to visit a retirement home where veterans live and another home for homeless veterans. I raised money to buy toiletries and grooming products. My mom and I brought baskets and made Easter gifts to deliver to the homes. I found out later that the veterans were very happy about receiving the gifts.

After doing more research, I learned about the Maryland Center for Veteran Education and Training (MCVET), and I took a tour. This nonprofit helps a lot of veterans, so I committed to donating a computer so the veterans could research jobs, backpacks, clothes, and toiletries. I changed the name of Give Back to Veterans Day to the Give Back to Veterans project, because I planned to do the project all year, not just one day.

The project has grown, and I became MCVET's superhero who raises money to pack what I call Hero Bags. These are filled with toiletries, clothes, underwear, t-shirts, kitchen items, shoes, socks, money, food cards, and whatever else veterans need. MCVET was able to receive 250 mattresses and pillows from Leesa Sleep and $1,000 donated in my name because the company picked me as a pint-sized change maker.

I even had an opportunity to talk to Steve Harvey on *Little Big Shots* about my project. I was awarded with a humanitarian award for season three. I now also go to other shelters and help even more veterans. My advice to children who are reading this is to keep going with whatever good you are trying to do. No matter what, don't give up!

Read a Story, Change a Life

Isabella Tejeda

I am a high school junior and an empowered changemaker. Three years ago, while volunteering at a local youth intervention camp for at-risk youth, I discovered that 78 percent of the students attending the camp were reading two grade levels below the California State Standards. Many of these children face daily obstacles such as poverty, language barriers, unstable homes, and peer pressure to join gangs. Some of the children shared with me that they were not "allowed" by their parents to check out books from the school library for fear of not being able to afford overdue or lost book fees. Armed with this information, I decided to create "Read a Story, Change a Life," a literacy intervention program designed to help promote literacy, inspire imagination, and build lifelong readers through storytelling and writing workshops.

I wanted to take what I learned from growing up at my local library and bring it to children who have not had the benefit of a similar experience. My program, which includes live puppet shows, interactive skits, songs, and writing workshops, is designed to empower these children to read and write their own stories. My program is now in partnership with Higher Ground Youth and Family Services, Lincoln Elementary, St. Joseph Primary School, and has been adopted by the Yorba Linda Public Library as an outreach program inspiring a love of reading throughout our community and beyond.

Our program services over 300 low-income families at Higher Ground, and now also services the residents of Oakcrest Terrace, a low-income community with an existing onsite preschool. A micro-grant from Karma 4 Cara enabled me to recreate the program, including the puppets, theater, story-time templates, books, and a self-produced instructional DVD, and ship it to the St. Joseph Primary School in Kampala, Uganda. Through grants and donations, I secured over five thousand dollars' worth of new books to start the HG Library; now the students at Higher Ground will have equal access to books and can take reading comprehension tests after school. We now have a team of over 120 volunteers, and this number is growing as the Reaching Higher Ground Club, which I founded at my school, and the Yorba Linda Library Teen Advisory membership continue to grow. We also won a one thousand dollar Pay It Forward Award from Disney Dreamers and Doers, which I donated to the tuition assistance fund at my school. After speaking and sharing "Read a Story, Change a Life" at my local National Charity League chapter meeting, the chapter chose Higher Ground Youth and Family Services as our 2019 philanthropy fundraiser recipients, resulting in a $37,000 donation to the Higher Ground Youth and Family Service intervention program.

My best advice for other young people who feel the desire to make a lasting change is to just go for it. Confidently and passionately put your idea out there, and don't take no for an answer—instead find your yes. I have learned that age does not define our ability to create lasting change in the world.

Photo Credit: Donna Reinbold

Make Someone Smile

Vincent Versaci

Doing good is a nice thing to do; it makes you happy. "Make someone smile, do a good deed, lend a hand to a friend in need" is a wise quote from the cuddly lamb Loukoumi. Loukoumi is a lamb who encounters different experiences in a series of books written by Nick Katsoris. In one book, Loukoumi needs a present for her dad's birthday, and she believes that she has to buy it. Her friends teach her that a gift is from the heart. Another book is about Loukoumi and a schoolyard bully, where she teaches the bully the Golden Rule. They become good friends. But this story is a story about me doing some good deeds.

Have you ever turned cans in for change at your local grocery store to help a charity? Well, I did, and when it's for a charitable reason, that's two things for one good deed. You get the experience of the job, and you donate to a good cause. For one of my good deeds, I asked people for bottles, plus I collected some of my own. I collected them and cashed them in for five cents each. I also went to a forest near where I live, and I picked up litter there. I got some money by recycling the bottles I collected! So, by picking up trash, I got money to donate. I donated it to The Loukoumi Foundation room at St. Jude Children's Research Hospital, and my school also donated.

Does your school make baskets for soldiers? Mine does. I went with my mom to the *Come From Away* show and my mom was inspired. In the show, a grateful guy whose plane was redirected to Newfoundland later gave his employees one hundred dollars to do good deeds. My mom did the same for my sister and me, telling us to write out our idea and show it to her, copying the good idea of the man in the show. I decided to use that money to make care baskets for soldiers. I bought candy and other things soldiers might want and need. I sent them to some soldier groups, and I included a card with each basket.

I enjoy going to Loukoumi fundraisers and events. I always go to the Loukoumi Make A Difference Bus Tour, and I usually go to the party after that at the Greek Church. I sell my blueberry jam, and I even sold some to a St. Jude worker. I always give half of my money that I make there to St. Jude and half to an animal shelter in Yonkers.

Charitable events and fundraisers are fun, and they are good for the community. They help others that don't have as much as you, and at the same time you can inspire others and do good yourself by donating money for good reasons! I hope you can get in on the action by donating or starting a fundraiser just like I did!

COME FROM AWAY
ESSAYS FROM GANDER

"How far that little candle throws his beams! So shines a good deed in a weary world."

William Shakespeare

Doing Good Deeds
from Gander, Newfoundland

On September 11, 2001, thirty-eight planes landed at the closest airport, which was Gander. All the passengers had to stay on the planes for twenty-four hours. Everyone in Gander did everything they could, bringing the passengers food, drinks, and blankets and trying to make them feel at home. This inspiring story from my community makes me want to do nice things for other people. And in my  school, doing nice things for other people is the golden rule.

One way I do nice things for others is to regularly go through my wardrobe and my toy bin and pick out things I don't want or use. I also give away some toys that I love. I put everything into a big bag and bring it to the Salvation Army. There they wash the clothing and toys to make sure they're clean so no one will get sick or have germs. They hang the clothes on nice, clean hangers and put the toys on shelves.

During the holidays, our school also collects food, water, toys, and clothing and we wrap them up in really pretty wrapping paper with big bows and put them under a tree in our school. We donate all the gifts to the Salvation Army, and one of the workers told us that we are really helping people in our community who don't have enough money to get toys or have a good big supper with their families. This made my classmates and me feel so happy!

—Chelsea Hynes

I'm proud of my community because they welcomed 7,000 strangers to Gander. About thirty-eight planes landed in the Gander Airport because the planes had to land in the closest airport on September 11, 2001.

Our town treated these passengers really well, and that encourages me to do the same. One thing I like to do is to make cards for my friends and give them treats. My sister is only three, so I like to help her get her toys that are hidden in her toy box and play with her.

Doing nice things for other people makes me feel happy. I like making people happy!

—Cooper Jones

If I had been alive when 9/11 happened, I would have tried to make things at least 1 percent better for the seven thousand people

stranded in our town. I would have donated bottles of water and some sort of food.

These days I share toys because it makes other kids feel good. Doing nice things for other people makes me feel good. Once I put a pair of PJs under a giving tree, and I hope the people that received them liked them.

Even when no one shares with me (which makes me sad), I still share with other people! I've donated snickerdoodles, chocolate chip cookies, and beans to the food bank. I like good deeds!

—Liam Vatcher

It makes me happy to know that Gander helped so many people to feel like they were part of the community when they were stranded here after 9/11. Even though I wasn't born yet, the *Come From Away* story inspires me to do good things.

One day my friends and I were playing dress up and really made a mess in my closet. We noticed that a lot of my clothes were way too small for us. That made me think about how some children hardly have any nice clothes to wear, and it made me feel sad. And then I had an idea . . . "Lillian, go grab some trash bags; Lily, you're on color-separation. I'll help Lily pack up the clothes into the bags. Go, go, go!" And that's when we started operation "HELP ALL IN NEED"!

I asked my mom if we could give my clothes to the less fortunate. She said yes. (Of course, she's the best mom ever!)

The next day my mom and I headed out to give the clothes to someone who needed them. It's the little things that count, and little things go quite a long way.

—Sydney Kellar

This year I went to New York. I saw the musical *Come from Away*. After it was over, I went to where the Twin Towers used to be. I am proud that my town helped during 9/11. I like helping people too.

At my primary school, we had a Christmas tree and we had to put stuff for animals under it. I brought dog food. Another time I was in my backyard and I found a bird stuck in my soccer net and I helped it get out. Doing good things makes me feel good.

—Joe Stratton

The 9/11 attacks were terrible. I wasn't born when the 9/11 attacks happened, but I know that Gander, my hometown, helped a lot. They gave out blankets to the people that needed them, gave them places to sleep, and most importantly, made sure that they were safe. If I had been alive then, I would've helped a lot too.

I like helping animals too. Once I found a frog and I took care of him before reuniting him with the other frogs.

—Amy Maddigan

Doing nice things for other people makes me happy. In school this past December, we donated to the food bank for people that don't have money to buy food. I brought a red Christmas bag with a snowman and a reindeer on it. Inside the bag there were a box of Fruit Loops and three cans of soup. I also brought five dollars to donate.

The next day the principal announced that 457 items had been donated. The day after that I saw even more people bring stuff to donate. I had a smile on my face every time I saw someone put something down. Bennett brought in a bag with five cans of soup, three packs of noodles, toys, and lots more. His bag was so heavy! As we put it under the tree, I looked at him and said, "Good job bringing in all this stuff for people!" We smiled the whole time we walked back to class.

I went to the food bank to get a tour of the building. The lady there told us a lot about it. We helped store the food in the back of the room, which was stuffed with food. When I left I thought to myself, *It feels so good to do something for someone else.* I can't wait until next year!

—Brady Chaulk-Goodyear

I love helping my friends and community. When I was little, one summer day my friend and I went for a bike ride. I said, "Do you see all that garbage? And do you want to pick it up?"

We went to my house to get rubber gloves and a plastic bag. We hopped on our bikes and went around and picked up a lot of garbage. We filled up our bike baskets and two garbage bags full of junk. We found things made of metal, plastic, and paper. There were a lot of juice boxes and straws, a lot of really wet paper. It was disgusting, but we kept on going until my friend had to go home.

After she left, I picked up even more garbage. It felt good helping the environment. I didn't like all the garbage I saw.

My dad told me I had to separate all the water bottles, and he told me what to pick up and what not to pick up. After supper I went to the school playground with my friend, and we picked up more garbage behind the school and behind people's houses. We had a lot of bags, and when we were done, we took them all to my house.

That night I thought about what I did. I was happy with myself, and I bet my friends were too. *We did a good thing,* I thought.

I know I wasn't born before 9/11, but I love helping everybody just as much as my town loved helping people back then. I was sad for the people that had to stay in the plane, but after I figured out that a lot of people helped out, I was happy.

We should all help out. Big or small, all shapes and sizes, enemy or friend, we all deserve a better world. Please make this world a better place!

—Lily Baker

Thinking of what Gander did during September 11th, 2001, inspires me to help people.

Doing good things for other people makes you and other people happy. In our school this past September, all of Gander Elementary did a Terry Fox Walk. It was a little bit long and even though my legs hurt, I still kept on walking because I knew it was a good deed. We gave our teacher money to donate to kids who have cancer. I donated twenty dollars, and that was the best day ever.

—Ciara Langdon

One time at my birthday party, I got three hundred fifty dollars. I spent most of the money at the mall in St. John's, and when I got home to Gander, I had fifty dollars left. I decided to do something nice for my mom and dad. I put it in an envelope and wrote a note with it, and then I gave it to my mom and dad. In the note I told my mom and dad how much they mean to me. I said how grateful I am to have a house and family like the one I have. They buy me stuff all the time, so that's the least I could do for them. My mom almost cried and that made me sad and happy at the same time. My dad was happy with me too.

My mom and dad tried to give it back to me, but I wouldn't let them. I think giving that money to my mom and dad was better than getting something out of it. I think doing good things is the best feeling!

—Ava Clarke

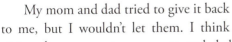

On September 11, 2001, thirty-eight planes landed in Gander, with 7,000 people on board. A lot of people stayed at my primary school, Gander Academy. Most of the people that had to stay in the school slept on the floor in classrooms and in the gym. A lot of the stores in Gander donated supplies such as toiletries, sleeping bags, and food.

Even though I wasn't there when it happened, I'm proud that my community helped everyone they could.

Doing nice things for people is very kind. My family often donates money to the Salvation Army for people who need it. Almost every Christmas, my friends and I donate stuff to the Salvation Army.

Most summers my sister and I, our two cousins, and my friend go around with clear garbage bags and clear blue recycling bags to pick up garbage and recycle cans. We picked up soda cans, napkins, plastic, and rotten food (which was really gross). But I loved doing it so much because I love to spend time with my friends, no matter what.

I also was in the "Swim for Hope," where you swim for people with cancer. My sister and I swam for our nana because she had cancer.

Doing good deeds is very good for everyone in your community!

—Sophie Angell

I am proud that my community helped people during 9/11. In November 2017, my family had an opportunity to help a man by letting him live in our house because he did not have a home of his own to stay in. We brought his two bags into the spare bedroom. After he got his clothes and stuff organized, we gave him some food because he was hungry.

He told us that he had to be at work soon, so we brought him to GFT, also known as Gander Flight Training. We picked him up after his workday was done, and we gave him food again.

My family also decided to give some of my toys to the second-hand store. It made a lot of sense because I had at least a thousand toys. I think the people who bought my toys would be very happy to play with my toys. It felt very good to share with people we didn't even know. Doing good deeds feels good!

—Dashiell Sharpe

I'm so proud to be from Gander because my community played a big part in helping people on September 11, 2001.

One Day in St. John's, my mom, my dad, my friend's dad and mom, and me were at Chapters on Kenmount Road. I found a cute brown-and-white stuffed cat that I thought that my friend Mackinley would love. I asked my mom if I could buy it because it's nice to do stuff (no pun intended) for other people. So we went up to the cashier and bought it.

—Bennett Knapman

Although I wasn't born until 2009, I know some things about 9/11 in Gander. My dad helped a lot because he has an important job at the airport. I know that thirty-eight planes and about 7,000 passengers had to land here, and the citizens of Gander helped them during their stay.

One day, if people need my help, I will help too. My dad and all the people that helped out during 9/11 will inspire me for the rest of my life. I will respect everyone too.

One day I was in St. John's. I was going to Toys"R"Us with fifty dollars I had gotten for my birthday, but then I saw someone on the street. He was wearing a torn shirt and old, messy pants. It was so sad. So I had an idea. It would be nice to get a toy, but I put that aside and asked my mom if I could go to Tim Hortons to get that man some food. I knew he wanted Tim Hortons because he was sitting next to the building. She said yes, so I got three coffees and donuts and muffins. The man was very happy when I gave it all to him. It was the best day of my life.

Life is amazing when someone cares about you. A little thing can make a big difference. Anyone can help! If you do, you will make a difference too.

—Jenna Wright

I am proud to live in Gander where *Come From Away* started, even though I was not born yet. People still remember that day, and my dad and I even watched a movie with some of the real "come from aways."

I like doing good deeds too. My friend goes to church and she told me that during Christmas she donated some food such as cereal, water, cans of soup and toiletries like toothbrushes, soap shampoo and brushes. I wanted to give to people in need, too, so I gave a lot of food, a toy, and some toiletries. It felt really good to give some things to people that need it even though I didn't have to.

I told my mom that I used my money to buy some things for people in need. She called the head of the church and told her what I did for poor people, and that person started to cry for joy. Now she and my mom are good friends. Her daughter is older than me. We are good friends too because of that too.

I asked my mom if I could go to church, and she said yes. I asked my mom if she would go with me. I said please so many times that she finally said yes. We both went to see if we liked it, and we did.

It just shows how a little thing can be huge, so if you have the chance to do something nice, I would take it!

—Sarah Pinhorn

Doing nice things for other people makes me happy. I love to give my clothes and toys to people that really need them. Last Christmas, I went through my toys and clothes so other kids could receive them for Christmas. I also gave a lot of my dolls. I gave away some of my clothes that didn't fit me. My mom was really proud of me!

—Mallory Coish

One time, I donated to the food bank with my class. We like raising money and donating to good causes. I gave a can of spaghetti and a box of Cheerios. I think the community liked that. I like doing the Terry Fox Walk every year. I also donated twenty dollars to Ninja's charity stream. He received over four thousand dollars because of nice people. There are a lot of things you can do to make a difference in the world. It doesn't matter what you have; it matters how you help others. It is always a good idea to do good deeds.

—Kaiden Hoffe

Once I was walking down the street with my best friend. It was a nice sunny summer day and we were just having fun. Then on the side of the sidewalk, we saw a butterfly with its wing ripped. I knew it must hurt a lot, so we picked it up and carried it to my friend's house.

Assuming it was attacked by a bird, it was barely moving. We dissolved some sugar in some water and soaked it up in a sponge and put it in the spare reptile enclosure I gave to my friend. The wind drifted in through the window as we put the butterfly in.

Every single day after that, I went to my friend's house to check on the butterfly. Eventually we constructed a fake wing and released the butterfly. To this day, my friend and I talk about this and wonder if the wing worked and if it lived. Now whenever we find injured animals, we attempt to help them. Helping others is the best.

—Kelson Blackmore

I like doing good things for other people. I like giving to people in need. I donate to the food bank. I give food like cereal, Kraft Dinner and a bunch of other stuff.

—Owen Barron

Doing nice things for people and animals is very kind and caring. One day when my sister broke my iPad, I had to stop her from throwing it in the trash. One time I was at Disney World and I went on the Kilimanjaro Safari ride in the Animal Kingdom, which is an adventure through the forest where you can see many animals that live in rain forests, and in the savanna, and even outback animals. The animals are there for visitors' enjoyment, but almost every animal is in there because it's an endangered species.

As the guide told us about the animals, she also explained how to help them. She said that the easiest and probably most helpful thing to do is to recycle. She mentioned that we could recycle electronic devices. So that's why when my sister broke my iPad, I had to stop her from throwing it in the trash and get her to put it in the recycling.

That night I went to bed feeling good because I had helped the environment. If everyone does their part in recycling, we can make the world a much better place for animals and us.

—Sawyer Ralph

In grade two, my class went on a trip to clean up around our school in our community of Gander. I went in a ditch because it was probably the spot with the most litter in Gander. Barely anybody would go down there since it was so dirty. My jumbo garbage bag was half-full and we were not close to being done.

Next we went into the woods. There was a lot more litter there than I expected. I found a very old, moldy banana; it was disgusting, but I picked it up and put it in the garbage anyway. I think keeping our community clean is important.

—Ben Barbour

On September 11, 2001, terrorists tried to knock down the Twin Towers in New York, and they succeeded. All the planes going to NYC had to land immediately. Thirty-eight planes landed in Gander, Newfoundland carrying 6,700 passengers. School buses picked up people from the airport and took them to the schools and the town hall and even people's houses  where they could stay. People were sleeping in classrooms and the gyms and on the floors, but they were comfortable and had warm blankets and sleeping bags. The citizens of Gander made cakes, casseroles, and good dinners for the passengers. The plane people were all trying to call home to talk to their family and friends, so Gander provided them with phones to call home. After it was over, the plane people were sad to leave.

—Graham Pittman

An Inspiring Role Model

Matthew and Nicholas Reda

Our dad, Gregory Reda, passed away on September 11th, 2001, when Nicholas was two-and-a-half years old and I was eight weeks old. Tuesday's Children is an organization that was formed to support young children who lost a parent on that day. One way they do this is by pairing up these children with mentors. These mentors are role models and volunteer their time to do activities with the children.

Nicholas was paired with Jim Giaccone when he was eight years old, and I joined in on the activities when I turned eight. Jim had lost his brother, Joseph Giaccone, on September 11th. To this day, Jim is a great match for Nicholas and me.

Jim is a thoughtful and generous man who has served as a great role model. He has taught us many lessons. He also shares interesting facts and tells hilarious jokes. The laughs and great memories we have had are too many to count. Jim is an extremely fun person to be around, and we always have a great time together. We have had so many new experiences that we are both extremely grateful for. We have done everything from fishing to bowling, launching rockets, building hovercrafts, paintballing, eating a lot, and going to the movies. Jim was even honored for his dedication to us by being a finalist for the 2016 NASCAR Humanitarian Award.

Jim has inspired Nicholas and me to volunteer our own time to help others. We have volunteered at many events hosted by our high school, St. Anthony's High School in South Huntington, as well as at various camps and programs for children with special needs. In addition, we have participated in volunteering events hosted by

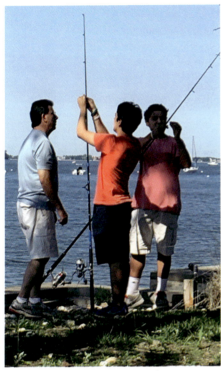

Photo courtesy of NASCAR Foundation

Tuesday's Children. For example, St. Anthony's High School hosts a Golden Kids Carnival and Friars Sports Camp, both which have games and activities for young kids with special needs. We have both also volunteered at Inclusive Sports and Fitness (ISF), a nonprofit organization that allows children with special needs to participate in various sports activities. We have run alongside them to encourage them to complete a 5K run. During Christmastime, we spend time with them so their parents can go holiday shopping. We know that both the children and their parents are grateful for this opportunity. We also volunteer as counselors at Esopus, a camp run by the Marist Brothers. Each session is a weeklong sleep-away camp for children or young adults with special needs. The week is filled with fun-filled activities.

With Tuesday's Children we have made blankets and care packages for veterans. Seeing the joy that we help bring to all of the children and young adults as well as the gratitude felt by the veterans makes volunteering extremely rewarding for us.

Watching Jim dedicate his time to us and Tuesday's Children has taught us to do the same in different ways. No matter how big or small, giving one's time back to the world and helping others will always make the world a better place.

ABOUT
COME FROM AWAY

Come From Away's journey began in 2011 when David Hein and Irene Sankoff (book and score) traveled to Newfoundland on the tenth anniversary of 9/11. While unsure what they were looking for, the incredible storytellers of Newfoundland shared numerous tales of ordinary people and extraordinary generosity that occurred during the week of 9/11 when 7,000 stranded passengers found a safe harbor in Newfoundland while the world around them was thrown into chaos. Inspired by the 16,000 stories they heard, they learned the importance of sharing tales about welcoming strangers and embracing kindness. The Tony and Olivier Award-winning musical they created has told, and continues to tell, the remarkable and uplifting true life story in productions on Broadway, in London, in Melbourne, in Toronto, and across North America in a multi-year tour.

Inspired by David and Irene's journey and the stories shared with them, *Come From Away* is proud to partner with The Loukoumi Foundation to publish the new book *Inspiring Stories That Make a Difference* encouraging children to generate their own acts of kindness and submit essays about their story and how they made a difference. The production is thrilled to be working with The Loukoumi Foundation to honor this next generation of storytellers and further its legacy of sharing stories of kindness that inspire the world to "pay it forward."

For more on *Come From Away*, please visit:
www.ComeFromAway.com

ABOUT
THE LOUKOUMI MAKE A DIFFERENCE FOUNDATION

Inspired by the Loukoumi children's book series by Nick Katsoris, The Loukoumi Make A Difference Foundation is a 501c3 nonprofit organization teaching children to make a difference in their lives and the lives of others. Starting in 2008 with the release of the book *Loukoumi's Good Deeds* narrated by Jennifer Aniston, the Loukoumi movement now unites over 100,000 children annually to do good deeds for causes that mean something to them. Children learn that good deeds can be fun as they make a difference in their own special way.

The Loukoumi Foundation has received the USA Weekend National Make A Difference Day Award, Tegna's Make A Difference Day All-Star Award, and The Point of Light Award. Based on this project, the Loukoumi Foundation sponsors The Make A Difference With Loukoumi Exhibit at The Westchester Children's Museum, a national literacy project benefiting St. Jude Children's Research Hospital and a Good Deed of the Month Curriculum in over 300 schools. The Loukoumi Foundation also sponsors its annual Dream Day contest, making kids' career dreams come true for a day. The Loukoumi programs were featured in the Make A Difference With Loukoumi TV Special that aired on FOX stations nationwide. The Foundation is honored to be teaming up with *Come From Away*, which tells the ultimate story of kindness, and with them looks forward to inspiring others to make a difference.

For more on The Loukoumi Foundation, please visit:
www.LoukoumiFoundation.org